TO BUILD JERUSALEM

A photographic remembrance of working class life, 1875-1950

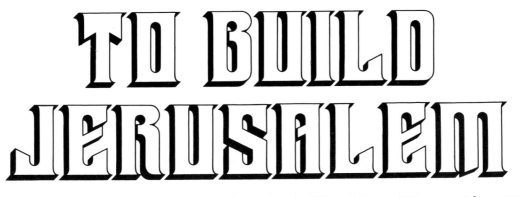

TO BUILD JERUSALEM

A Photographic Remembrance of British Working Class Life 1875-1950

JOHN GORMAN

Though the way seem often doubtful,
Hard the toil which we endure,
Though at times our courage falter,
Yet the promised land is sure.

Clarion Hymn

Scorpion Publications London

First published in 1980 by Scorpion Publications Ltd

ISBN 0 905906 26 8 cased
ISBN 0 905906 27 6 paperback

Editor: Leonard Harrow
Design and Production: Colin Larkin
Art Editor: John Gorman
Design Assistant: Rhonda Larkin
Set In Plantin 110
Printed on Huntsman Velvet 135 gsm
Printed in England by W S Cowell Ltd, Ipswich, Suffolk

To Jon, my son

In the grave where tyrants thrust them,
*   lies their labour and their pain,*
But undying from their sorrow
*   springeth up the hope again.*

William Morris

Contents

Photographic Acknowledgements

p. 2 **Mill girl**, C. Kemp
p. 6 **Young miner**, North of England Open Air Museum
p. 10 **Washer woman**, Manchester Studies/Francis Prendiville
p. 12 **Engineers**, John Gorman Collection
p. 14 **Girl in bath**, Joe Short
p. 16 **Pickets**, Association of Scientific, Technical and Managerial Staffs
p. 19 **Children shovelling coal**, Joe Short
p. 23 **West Riding police**, Miss A. Wilkinson
p. 25 **Speaker with red flag**, John Gorman Collection
p. 27 **Young miner**, North of England Open Air Museum
p. 30 **Coalies**, Jon Gorman
p. 31 **Limeburners/Greenwich**, Greenwich Local History Library
p. 32 **Carpenters/Carnoustie**, John Gorman Collection
p. 33 **Eviction/Cherhill**, National Union of Agricultural and Allied Workers
p. 34 **Railwaymen/LB & SCR**, National Railway Museum
p. 35 **Railwaymen/Fence Houses**, National Railway Museum
p. 36 **Coal trimmers**, North of England Open Air Museum
p. 37 **Factory explosion/Cornbrook**, C. E. Makepeace
p. 38 **Aqueduct builders/Thirlmere**, C. E. Makepeace
p. 39 **Manchester Ship Canal**, C. E. Makepeace
p. 40 **Pitbrow lasses**, H. M. Trett
p. 41 **Opening of Woolwich Ferry**, Greenwich Local History Library
p. 42 **Dock strike/feeding children**, H. J. Pugh
p. 43 **End of dock strike**, Ron Todd
p. 44 **Hedger**, Museum of Rural Life
p. 45 **Harvester**, Museum of Rural Life
p. 46 **Royal Oak keel laying**, John Gorman Collection
p. 47 **Coopers/Sussex**, Museum of Rural Life
p. 48 **Cavalry/Wentworth**, Brian O'Malley Central Library and Arts Centre, Rotherham
p. 49 **Pleasley Colliery**, Glyn Jones
p. 50 **Mersey carters**, Ken Sprague
p. 51 **Miners/Ty Tryst**, Glyn B. Davies
p. 52 **Ragged School**, North of England Open Air Museum
p. 53 **Cotton spinners**, S. Healey
p. 54 **Farthing breakfast queue**, Salvation Army
p. 55 **Farthing breakfast**, Salvation Army
p. 56 **John Pearson**, R. F. Jones
p. 57 **Mafeking celebration/Enfield**, Enfield Central Library
p. 58 **Living-in demonstration**, John Gorman Collection/ *Reynolds News*
p. 59 **Destitute women/Embankment**, H. J. Pugh
p. 60 **Coffin beds**, Salvation Army
p. 61 **Wash and brush up**, H. J. Pugh
p. 62 **Children in playground**, Fawcett Library
p. 63 **Children at pieshop**, Salvation Army

p. 64 **Slum children**, Salvation Army
p. 65 **Children with pushchair**, H. J. Pugh
p. 66 **Children chopping firewood**, Central Library, Manchester
p. 67 **Washing the flags**, C. E. Makepeace
p. 68 **Carrow School**, Colman Foods
p. 69 **Men leaving work**, Colman Foods
p. 70 **Women brickmakers**, John Gorman Collection
p. 71 **Chainmakers**, Black Country Society
p. 72 **Metal shearing**, C. E. Makepeace
p. 73 **Tramway laying**, L. F. Barham
p. 74 **Raunds march**, R. E. Jones
p. 75 **Raunds march**, R. F. Jones
p. 76 **Leicester march**, Newarke Houses Museum
p. 77 **Marchers washing**, Newarke Houses Museum
p. 78 **Knocking-up**, C. Kemp
p. 78 **Mill girls**, C. Kemp
p. 80 **Ernest Marklew**, L. H. Wilkinson
p. 81 **Unemployed demonstration/Manchester Cathedral**, Central Library, Manchester
p. 82 **Caslon workshop**, John Gorman Collection
p. 83 **By-election, Haggerston**, H. J. Pugh
p. 84 **Ned Page**, North of England Open Air Museum
p. 85 **Stanley pit disaster funeral**, North of England Open Air Museum
p. 86 **Wounded soldier**, Hulton Picture Library
p. 87 **Durham mining family**, North of England Open Air Museum
p. 88 **Radcliffe Co-op**, Co-operative Union
p. 89 **Lord Mayor's goodbye**, C. E. Makepeace
p. 90 **Tom Mann**, source unknown
p. 91 **Soldiers and striker**, Ken Sprague
p. 92 **Rail strike, Clapham**, National Railway Museum
p. 93 **Women's strike**, Ken Sprague
p. 94 **Herring strikers**, North of England Open Air Museum
p. 95 **Women drinking**, North of England Open Air Museum
p. 96 **Street scene**, Sid Brown
p. 97 **Clarion van**, Michael Katanka
p. 98 **Builders' strike**, Ken Sprague
p. 99 **Recruiting**, Radio Times Hulton Picture Library
p.100 **Women engineers**, Central Library, Manchester
p.101 **Woman gas workers**, North Thames Gas
p.102 **Horseflesh shop**, Newarke Houses Museum
p.103 **Wounded soldier**, Newarke Houses Museum
p.104 **Pig killing**, North of England Open Air Museum
p.105 **Leek show/Castleside**, North of England Open Air Museum
p.106 **Domestic servants**, Manchester Studies/Bessie Goodwin
p.107 **Domestic training**, Fawcett Library

Acknowledgements

Many people have given generously of their time and help throughout the various stages in the shaping of this book and it is not possible to acknowledge them all individually. I am particularly indebted to Sid Brown, a good comrade and friend, for his constant willingness to dig out information, offer constructive advice and stimulate new thoughts over a pint of Burton. I am grateful also to Eve Denney for her immaculate typing of my manuscript and her extraordinary ability to decipher my handwriting; also to Pat Richmond, who typed my continuous correspondence. Peter J. Dixon shared my enthusiasm for the project and gave invaluable professional advice on layout and design, though circumstances led the final production in another direction. I was helped in the beginning of my research by Monica Allen and Karen Jacobs and missed them both as I plodded through the rest alone. My thanks are due to the trade union journals and socialist publications that printed my appeal for photographs and above all to the hundreds of working people, trade unions, trades councils and constituency Labour Parties who entrusted to me their precious photographs, the majority of which could not be included for reasons of space.

I was sustained in my work by the compliance of my wife, Pamela, who was abandoned by me for endless weekends and evenings while I was searching, sifting and writing. On too many occasions she was deprived of her favourite Saturday morning coffee in Sagne's.

Finally, my thanks are due to the librarians, curators and staffs of the following libraries, museums and organisations, who received me with courtesy and gave expert assistance: Birmingham Reference Library, Black Country Society, British Library, Newspaper Library, Colindale, Burnley District Central Library, Colman's Foods, Copeland Borough Council, Co-operative Union, Cornwall County Council, Dudley Public Library, Enfield Central Library, Fawcett Library, Greater London Council, Hamilton District Museum, Imperial War Museum, Loughton Public Library, Manchester Central Library, Manchester Studies Unit, Marx Memorial Library, Mitchell Library, Glasgow, *Morning Star*, Museum of Rural Life, National Coal Board, National Railway Museum, Negas, Nelson District Central Library, Newarke Houses Museum, Leicester, Northampton Central Museum, North Thames Gas, North of England Open Air Museum, Oldham Library, Rotherham Central Library, Salvation Army, South Shields Central Library, Stafford County Education Office, Tower Hamlets' Central Library, Working Class Movement Library, Manchester.

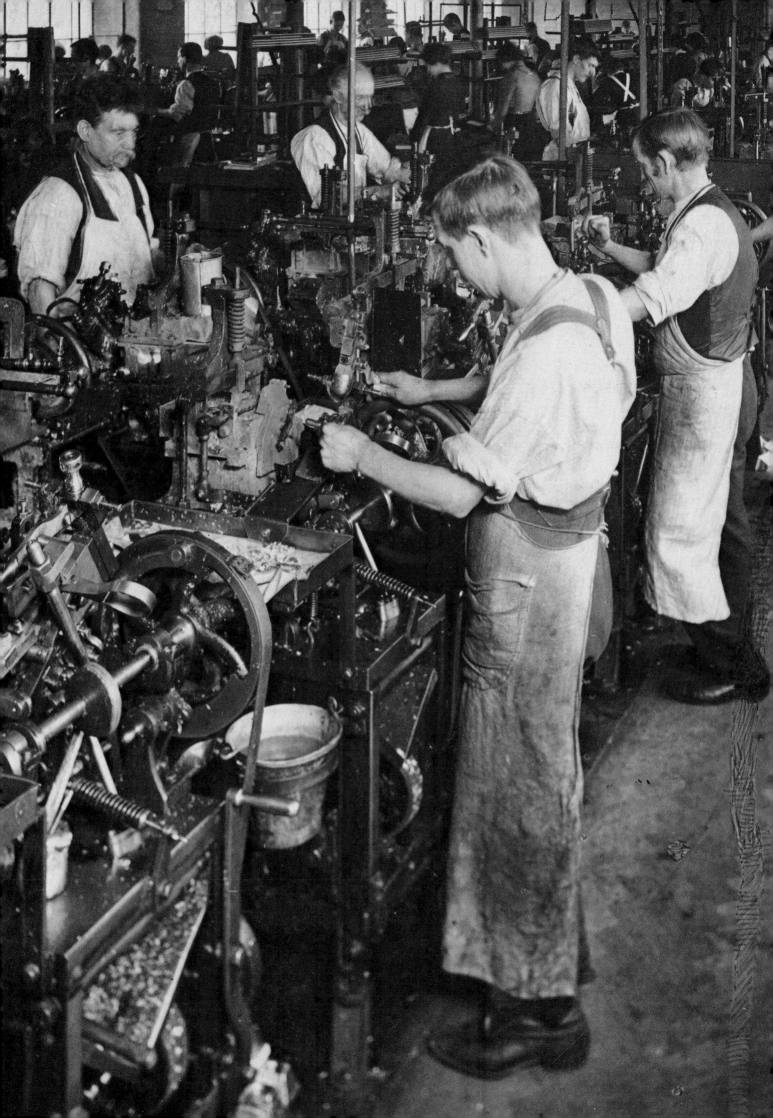

Foreword

John Gorman's first book, on trade union banners, has become a necessary text for anyone who wants to understand the development of the Trade Union and Labour Movement. In this second book he has taken a broader and more controversial scene, but one that is no less fascinating or important. The camera was of course invented and developed too late to portray the earliest 19th century developments of the Trade Union Movement but fortunately was in sufficiently wide use from the 1870s onwards to portray the vital trade union initiatives of those days.

Of the photographs that are reproduced here, few have been seen outside the albums or cupboards of those who collected them. Hardly any have been previously published. They illustrate the connection between the conditions faced by the ordinary people of Britain and the development of the organisations that those people created to better their intolerable circumstances. The photographs in this book remind us vividly of the need to ensure that nobody throws away photographs of working people. These living records of yesterday may often help us to understand the problems of today and tomorrow.

In order to appreciate the value of this fascinating pictorial history which John Gorman has assembled, the reader does not have to agree with every point of his description, selection or analysis. I don't myself. The debate about the Trade Union Movement's—and the TUC's—response to the General Strike, unemployment in the 1930s and international problems then and later will no doubt continue.

It is a stimulating, often inspiring, collection of photographs, assiduously collected and selected, which brings alive a major aspect of British history over a large part of the last century. It has, of course, never been true that the camera cannot lie: but it can help to illuminate the truth. This is what John Gorman has done.

LIONEL MURRAY

Introduction

Any selection of photographs is necessarily purposeful and subjective and this collection has been shaped by the memories and experience of a working class childhood, of poverty and craft pride, of family loyalty and class solidarity, the personal witness of the destructiveness of violence and the traumatic consequences of growing up in a society based on competition and the private acquisition of wealth. In the construction of this brief visual remembrance of working class life the source has often been as important as technical quality, aesthetic value or historical validity, a snapshot as vital as the work of the photo journalist or studio photographer, and a deeply etched belief in the essential humanity of the cause of organised labour central to the expression of the portrayal and the memory.

Those photographs which are culled from the albums, wallets and mantelpieces of working people are of especial significance, treasured as they have been over the years as graphic proof of past shared experience. The photograph of building workers marching in support of the miners in the General Strike of 1926 (p.122) shows the leading figure marked with a cross, 'that is my father,' wrote E. G. W. Horley from Leamington Spa, 'he worked with Bradfords, a firm of builders in Mill Street' and then added without further comment, 'I was made redundant with the same firm on Good Friday of this year after forty-six years' service.' His creased and tattered card becomes as evidence in the indictment of capitalism. There is a cross too on the picture of hunger marchers from Wales in 1936, lining up outside a Camberwell school (p.154) early in the morning, ready for the final lap of their journey to London; it marks the figure of Amos Mouls, another building worker and later secretary of the Swansea Trades Council. It is a melancholy scene, the men marshalled to the side of the road by officious police, a worker in the foreground, cap in hand, and two of the marchers raising their clenched fists in the salute of the Popular Front, an act of assertion and defiance as they stand to be counted for posterity by the cameraman. The corner of the photograph is missing, but for Amos Mouls the memory and bitterness of those hungry years is intact and revived each time the picture is handed around. Such pictures are a personal witness and represent a crucial part of the visual history of the labour movement as important as banners, badges, emblems and other pictorial memorabilia. Viewed as historical documents they should be conserved as carefully as minute books and diaries for they stem from the very roots of the movement, from the people themselves.

Characteristic of these photographs is the collection of R. J. Short, a worker photographer who has spent forty years of his life as a miner, starting work at Houghton Colliery in 1916 at the age of thirteen. An enthusiastic photographer since 1923, his pictures of working class life in the Barnsley area of Yorkshire, extending over a period of more than fifty years have an instinctive insight and feeling that derives from having been part of that life. The picture of children bathing (p. 14) is a memory of his past immediately understandable to the millions who share the childhood memory of a zinc bath in front of the fire, of water softened with soda and the thin lather of brick hard soap. The children are his sisters, Rosie in the bath, Emily sitting on the sofa already scrubbed, and Sarah, out of focus because she did not want her picture taken. The photograph was taken in 1926 with his first camera, a Kodak Autographic, and the bath is the one that Joe Short, his father, and his three brothers also used after coming home from work at the pit. After bathing they would spread their damp pit clothes in front of the fire to dry out, ready to put on again at 4 a.m. the next morning. They always shook their clothes before dressing to shake out the black beetles that crawled in during the night to share the blackness and damp warmth. On summer evenings Joe would sit with the door open to the backyard and shoot the 'black-clocks' with an air gun as they crawled over the step. A familiar scene in any mining community was the delivery of the miners' coal allowance (often mistakenly referred to as free coal) dropped at the backyard or front door, and the house in the photograph (p. 19) is where the Short family lived in Station Road, Wombwell, in 1935. The cast iron railings and short-trousered boys clearly stamp the period before the Second World War and the two lads, Arthur Lindley and Stan Shields, are seen giving a hand with shovelling the fuel into the coal hole. Short's photographs taken during the General Strike and lock-out of 1926, a few of which are included in this miscellany (pp. 131, 132, 133) are taken by a man at once photographer and striker, an unusual combination more than half a century ago before mass produced roll-film instant cameras made photographers of us all. While the photographers of Fleet Street were dutifully serving their Press Lords with pictures of Fair Isle jumpered undergraduates driving buses and debutantes making tea, Short was taking what he saw where he lived, miners distributing bread for the children from the Working Men's Club, running soup kitchens and selling cheap fish in a valiant attempt to combat the starvation being forced upon them by intransigent mineowners and a hostile government.

Another miner photographer, whose work was found during the search for material towards the compilation of this book, was James Anderson of Methil, Fife. His album of one hundred photographs taken during the General Strike was given by his wife after his death to Tom Cordiner, secretary of the Levenmouth Trades Council. The album is a rare record of the strike and lock-out in a single mining community and vividly portrays the social and political life of the miners and their families during the long struggle. The yellowing prints are not of the highest technical quality but collectively make a valuable contribution to our understanding of that momentous event. The album includes not only pictures of soup kitchen workers and fancy dress fund raising, both common subjects of General Strike photographs, but ranges from interior and exterior shots of miners' cottages, local strike leaders, the action committee, women pit-head workers, empty coal wagons at Wellesley Colliery, the miners

march from East Wemyss to Thornton and the arrest of pickets at Muiredge, to scenes of miners relaxing in the open air, giving a concert, wrestling and playing football.

In a different category, an official documentary photographic record of the arrest, imprisonment and release of the Poplar Borough Councillors in 1921 is contained in the presentation albums given to the convicted members of the Council in 1922. Each of the thirty Labour men and women who were imprisoned, the mayor, four aldermen and twenty-five councillors, was presented at a meeting of the Council held on 9 November 1922 with a bound and hand-lettered photographic record of their courageous fight for the poor. Forty-nine pictures recall the widespread enthusiastic support given by Poplar workers and workless to their Council in its refusal to cut the poor relief or raise the rates in a borough overburdened with unemployed and slum housing. Starting with a photograph of the Council in session on 22 March 1921, when they voted to refuse to levy the precepts of outside authority, mainly the London County Council, the album is packed with scenes of the momentous struggle that followed. The mayor, Sam March, wearing his chain of office and accompanied by the macebearer is shown leading the march of the Council beneath a banner carrying the message 'Poplar Borough Council marching to the High Court and possibly to prison'. Behind them came thousands of supporters and the flowing silken banners of the London stevedores and dockers. There follow pictures of some of the councillors, the serving of summons, mass meetings of support and the

farewell from the people as they escorted their councillors to the borough boundary, bands playing and banners flying as they were taken to Brixton and Holloway. A woman is pictured rushing forward to shake hands with Minnie Lansbury as she was taken away. Alderman Susan Lawrence tells the crowd 'women are not afraid of prison' and the captions race through the events, 'three cheers for Poplar' and 'stone walls do not a prison make nor iron bars a cage' as the councillors say goodbye. There are close-ups of sections of the fifteen thousand strong procession that marched to Holloway on the first day of the imprisonment of the women councillors, at their head the historic dockers' banner, Union and Victory. The men councillors are photographed outside Brixton Prison upon their release, having walked through the gates to freedom singing The Red Flag to a hero's welcome from thousands. There are pictures of the masses in Newby Place awaiting the arrival of the women councillors upon their release and of the triumphant victory rally held in Victoria Park. Among the banners of support can be seen the rare sight of the standard of K Branch of the National Union of Police and Prison Officers next to the banner of the Poplar Trades' Council proclaiming the 'solidarity of labour'.

The album from which the two photographs included in this collection (pp. 114, 115) were taken, was presented to the deputy mayor, Charles Sumner, and loaned by his son Stephen, a member of the Woodford Labour Party. The selected pictures show not the leaders of the revolt but the sort of people for whom the Council fought, the poor people so beloved by George Lansbury, the instigator of the revolt, the gentle Christian socialist who was in turn so loved by his people of Poplar.

By contrast and in contradiction to my intent, a few photographs of working class interest are included in the collection that originate from business companies. The photograph of boy workers in the brass rule department of the Caslon Letter Foundry (p.82) is one of a series of thirty-four pictures taken by Reinhold Thiel & Company for Caslon's at the turn of the last century. The photographs, bought in a sale room, depict every activity of the company in the making of type except punch cutting which was one of the mysteries of the craft. Admittedly the workshops have been tidied up and the operatives are smart and posed but there is a myriad detail of factory and office life of the period to be gleaned from close study. Tools, clothes, the work of women, the sharp division between office staff and factory workers and between supervisors and supervised reveals more than was intended at the time. Likewise the unconscious class difference is alarmingly apparent in the photograph of the shearing machine operator and his employers in the picture taken for Henry Gittus at the Midland Iron Works (p.72). Both photographs provide an insight into workshop life that was never in the eye of the photographer.

A valuable source of little known and probably unpublished photographs originating from the labour movement has been the discovery of an old box of lantern slides produced for propaganda lectures by the Social Democratic Federation. These were found at Southend-on-Sea in the possession of a former member of the British Socialist Party, Herbert Pugh, a life-long fighter for the cause of socialism. The thirty chipped and cracked slides date from about 1906 and include a picture from the great dock strike of 1889 and the SDF organised unemployed demonstrations of 1905. The Democratic Federation was founded in 1881 by Henry Meyers Hyndman, a prosperous old Etonian, who played first class cricket for Sussex and who upset Karl Marx by writing England For All, a book of unacknowledged Marxian inspiration. A radical group, the Democratic Federation became committed to the cause of socialism in 1884, changing its name to the Social Democratic Federation and changing it again in 1908 to the Social Democratic Party. The lantern slides are a mixture of photographs, cartoons and song words; the photographs depict unemployed workers, destitutes, night refuges, political meetings and demonstrations. The cartoons include one by Walter Crane, the talented socialist artist who joined the SDF after his friend, William Morris, had introduced him to the 'Cause'. The iconography of the drawing is typical of Crane, with a female figure wearing a cap of liberty, holding a banner and a garland, the inscription on the banner reading 'All roads lead to Socialism'. A winding army of workers bear banners with the slogans of the day, 'Feed the children', 'A commonwealth when wealth is common', 'Work for all', 'Pensions for old age' and the controversial SDF demand for a Citizen Army. The photographs of poverty, destitute women on the embankment (p.59), Manchester unemployed sitting aimlessly by park railings and a Christmas scene in a refuge for the homeless contrast savagely with an interior shot of a luxurious hotel, the dining-room set for a banquet at sixty pounds a head, and a picture of a single crystal vase sold in London for £15,525, the slide captioned 'one of the causes of poverty'. Unfortunately most of the captions are missing and a good deal of research was required to identify the election picture at Haggerston, East London (p.83), and the demonstration of the unemployed in Berkeley Square (p.79). Some of the slide pictures remain unidentified.

The purpose of this collection has not been to present a chronological visual history but to create a keepsake impression of the life and times of the organised working class, using, wherever possible, images drawn from the homes of people who have shared in the building of the labour movement. For that reason historically important photographs have sometimes been passed over in favour of the seemingly secondary, a group photograph of the Hammersmith Socialist League offered by the Victoria and Albert Museum yielding place to a group photograph of Wigan pit brow lasses (p.40) sent by Mrs Trett, great grand-daughter of the overseer, the famous picture of the Jarrow Crusade displaced by a snapshot of Scottish hunger marchers sent by veteran trade unionist, Bill McQuilkin of Paisley. Few people will be familiar with the life of William Hodgman (p.134) but at eighty-three years of age he was to write of his regret at no longer being able to take an active part in the fight against unemployment. This message from a hardened campaigner of the unemployed struggles of the thirties, a trade unionist and agitator since boyhood, weakened in body but not in faculty or spirit, compelled the inclusion of his precious photograph as a tribute to the selfless dedication of thousands like him, unknown and tireless workers for the ideals of trade unionism and socialism.

Where it has not been possible to find individuals with photographs to cover a period, I have turned to libraries and museums, often with specialist collections, to complete the composite picture. Here, I have sought to avoid the familiar photographs and searched for the obscure which have often been donated by ordinary working people, a circumstance particularly true of the photographs used from the collection of the North of England Open Air Museum and of Manchester Studies. In the final analysis, the choice has been personal. If certain trades and occupations are un-represented it is regretted, for they are all part of the great army of labour. If there is a disproportionate number of photographs of miners and mining life it is because the miners have been the shock troops of labour's army, in the vanguard of struggle and too often the first target for assault.

Omissions and limitations are therefore acknowledged and accepted. Notable events in the building of trade unionism may be missing for other reasons, perhaps they were never recorded on glass or film, perhaps as in the instance of the historic struggle for the eight hour day at Beckton Gas Works in 1888, an exhaustive search failed to produce a single photograph. The first May Day march in London, 1890, seems to have passed unrecorded by the camera as did the massive unemployment demonstrations of 1886 and 1887, but some remarkable photographs of the great dock strike of 1889 survive and here again the unfamiliar has been used instead of the better known. The photograph of the triumphant end to the strike (p.43) was discovered in West Ham (now Newham) by Ron Todd, National Organiser of the Transport and General Workers' Union, the union that stems directly from the heroic revolt of the London dockers. The scene of women and children being fed in the street is a print made from one of the SDF lantern slides. Other crucial events are to be found wanting for no better reason than lack of space, the ordinary frequently squeezing out the extraordinary.

The photographs related to leisure gave balance to the picture of working class life, for even in the hardest times, there was always humour and if the good times were fewer than they are today, they were never totally non-existent. The charabanc outing of women workers of the North Kensington Labour Party (p.117), sent by Joan Davies of the Epping Labour Party, is a lovely remembrance of day trips before the mass production of the motor car, and if 'hopping' was hardly a holiday (p.159) it was certainly regarded as a treat by the kids and was an escape from the soot of the city. The gargantuan mixture of beer, beano, bands and banners of the Durham Miners' Gala was unquestionably an expression of solidarity, it was also for most the only real outing of the year, and the glorious photograph of the family scene at the 1937 Gala (p.163) printed from an old glass negative from *Reynolds News*, beautifully captures the happiness of the moment.

It has been necessary also to show something of the humiliation, the degradation and poverty that was inflicted upon millions of our citizens by the ruling class of the richest empire the world had known. If the sight of men sleeping in coffin-like beds (p.60) is a shock, it is matched for poignancy by the photographic record of council officials fumigating bedding (p.157). It serves no purpose to pretend that lice, bed-bugs and cockroaches did not share the lives of working people condemned to live in the slums of private landlordism, for the shame belongs to the rich, not to the poor. If the ignominy of the inquisition of the means test has escaped the lens, the gaunt staring poverty of the thirties is constantly revealed in the eyes of the unemployed. The memory of the face of the out of work

man clutching the 'hand out' of a mug of hot tea (p.140) lingers in the mind, to be recalled again and again, disturbing the conscience. These are pictures of the price of capitalism, of hunger in a land of silent factories and fallow fields, of unmitigated misery in a land of industrial skills and natural wealth. Revealed also is the determination to challenge the iniquity of an unjust society, the courage to fight back against oppression, the capacity of ordinary people to organise against state power, the refusal to be coerced by troops, employers, police or petty officials. From the faded photographs of hungry children, of eviction and lock-outs, of marches, strikes and demonstrations, of work, war and struggle, emerges the constant hope, the passion and the promise of a better life for all people.

The starting point of 1895 was forced largely by circumstance, for photographic records of working class life prior to that date are rare and the portrayal of labour invariably romantic. The choice of 1950 at which to close the album does have significance, for it is a watershed in the folk memory of a living generation that lived through the blind and bloody brutality of capitalism from the time of the First World War, to rejoice in the apparent millennial realisation of working class power in 1945 and the first five years of real Labour rule.

As a collection, the photographs show us something of the lives and circumstances of the people that built the labour movement, our fathers, grandfathers and their fathers who fought on immediate issues and yet never lost the vision and the promise of a new Jerusalem. The effect of light on silver salts may never have been conceived as a weapon in the class struggle but photographs are a two dimensional aid to the better understanding of our three dimensional world and their comprehension can provide a stimulus to action. Whatever the limitations of the frozen image, contrived, posed, selected or cropped to suit the eye of the manipulator, there is still value to be extracted by the critical viewer. Dwelling over images that recollect our past gives us cause to be thankful that, for whatever reason, somebody thought the occasion worthy of remembrance.

Early acknowledgement of calculated remembrance must be made to the enterprise of the secretary of the Salisbury District of the National Agricultural Labourers' Union, A. Smee, who responded to the news of the eviction of three of his members from Cherhill in 1876 by commissioning a 'first rate photographer' to record the aftermath of the event. Tripod and plate camera were rushed by horse and trap to the village and the evicted family with their few possessions were posed at the hedgerow before their former home. Smee must have had a positive flair for publicity for the resulting photographs were sold as cartes-de-visite for sixpence each and cabinet size for a shilling, the proceeds being used to aid the victims and the union. The story of the eviction is a tale of tyranny in the countryside, of feudal power and the refusal of an agricultural labourer to bow to the will of a trade union hating squire.

The NALU had been formed in 1872 by Joseph Arch, the son of a Warwickshire shepherd, and despite internal division was more than fifty-eight thousand strong in 1875 and organised into thirty-eight districts. Opposition from the farmers and landed gentry was fierce and the agricultural workers scattered in isolated villages were extremely vulnerable to the absolute power of a hostile squirarchy. In the village of Cherhill, power was wielded by Squire Heneage and his family who owned virtually the entire village and much of the surrounding land. The squire's wife was always ready to upbraid any woman of the labouring class who might dress above her station in life and interfered in proposed marriages of which she did not approve. Any girl who 'transgressed' was not allowed to stay at home and had to be driven out, as in a Victorian melodrama. When William Durham, an agricultural labourer of Cherhill, together with his two sons joined Arch's union, they were in effect challenging the rule of the squire. To compound the heresy, Durham, a man of integrity and independence, did not support the established Church but was a Wesleyan. In arranging the eviction photograph E. W. Sanger, the photographer, was careful to display Durham's framed poster of Joseph Arch and a collecting box for the Wesleyan Missionary Society among the effects.

Durham had lived in the Heneage-owned cottage for twenty-eight years and was known in the district as a sober and industrious worker but his support for the union was not to be tolerated and after a court order had been obtained the Durham family were ejected by the police. A week later the Durhams' twelve year old daughter was turned out of the village school, a measure of the callous and petty vindictiveness of the English gentry. The union rallied to suport Durham and the NALU held a joint rally with the *English Labourer* in a field at Cherhill, lent by a Mr John Clark. In pouring rain a thousand people sang 'When Arch Beneath The Wellesbourne Tree', a stirring union song, but despite the brave words the majority of the people were afraid of losing their homes and had to concede defeat to the Heneages.

In the cities the same open hostility and suspicion prevailed towards the developing trade unions who were viewed by Victorian employers as a threat to the nicely arranged natural order of society, each in his place. Nowhere was this regimental order better reflected than in the photographs taken for the local and national railways that flourished in the 1880s (pp.34,35). From north to south, the railwaymen are shown uniformed, grouped and graded in outward confirmation of established order from top-hatted station master through brass-buttoned ticket collectors to the lowliest van boy. Indeed, the very name of the Amalgamated Society of Railway Servants, founded in 1872, buttresses the concept of a society based on masters and servants. Behind the rows of liveried staff paraded on platforms is concealed the harsh discipline, unpaid overtime, excessive hours of work and physical danger that was the reality of working for independent railway companies. They were run like private armies and the manager of the London and North Western Railway expressed his opinion in 1893 that 'you might as well have trade unionism in Her Majesty's army as have it in the railway service.' It was this reactionary and stiff-necked attitude that was to lead to the historic strike of railwaymen at Taff Vale in August 1900. The chairman of the Taff Vale Railway Company, R. L. G. Vassal, was already 'most decidedly' of the opinion that 'trade unions were a very pernicious body as regards railway companies.' In a strike precipitated by the victimisation of a signalman who was a leading member of the ASRS, combined with a claim for higher wages, the company evicted all their employees who occupied railway cottages, brought in blackleg labour and successfully sued the union for damages of £23,000. By

holding the union responsible for losses incurred by actions arising from the strike, the Law Lords overturned what seemed to be the explicit provisions of the Trade Union Acts of 1871-6 and made strikes nearly impossible. The judgement proved to be a decisive contribution to the formation of the Labour Party, helping to convince the trade unions of the necessity of being represented in Parliament. The affiliated membership of the Labour Representation Committee, formed in 1900, rose from 375,930 to 969,800 by 1903 and by 1906 twenty-nine Labour MPs had been returned to Parliament.

While bowler-hatted craft-skilled trade unionists like those seen with their giant painted banner at the opening of the Woolwich Free Ferry in 1889 (p.41) enjoyed a measure of respectability and a regular wage, the so-called unskilled lived a precarious existence. Balanced between poverty and absolute destitution they were feared by the middle class and despised by skilled and organised trade unionists. At the bottom of the social heap were the casual labourers, thousands of whom daily fought for work at the gates of London's docks. Ben Tillett, founder of the Tea Operatives and General Labourers' Association, precursor of the Dockers' Union, told how these men 'lived more by accident than by design', 'picking over the rubbish heaps in search of anything eatable' and of the 'furtive storing of refuse rice the coolies had thrown away'. The manager of the Millwall Docks gave evidence at an enquiry, of men who came to work without a scrap of food in their stomachs and gave up after an hour, their hunger not allowing them to continue. They were, said Tillett, 'Lazaruses who starve upon crumbs from the rich man's table.'

The story of the strike for the 'dockers' tanner' is legendary and the engravings from *The Illustrated London News* of 1889 and a few contemporary photographs of the strikers are familiar enough. However, the photograph from the SDF lantern slide set, entitled 'women and children of dock strikers being fed in the street' (p.42), does not appear to have been previously published. The photograph of the women with their babies, clearly shows the relief tickets issued to strikers pinned to their dresses and hats. Unfortunately the location is unidentified, but we do know that the first relief tickets were issued under the control of Tom Mann from the dingy little Wroot's Coffee House and later during the strike from eight distribution centres in the East End of London. The tickets, issued by the union, were exchangeable for food from local traders and the system of relief helped to sustain the strikers and their families and build the union during the month-long struggle. The photograph is a rare relic from that epic fight which heralded the 'new unionism' and the organisation of the unskilled.

The large card-mounted photograph, size 270 × 310mm (p.49), of police at Pleasley Colliery, taken during the great lock-out of 1893, confirms the accounts of the widespread dispersal of police forces against the miners during that savage and deadly dispute. Pleasley is in Nottinghamshire and the police in the photograph are constables from Montgomery County force, the photograph being found in an attic in Welshpool during a house clearance and given to a local police officer, Detective Sergeant T. Victor Jones. It was the policy of Asquith, Home Secretary at the time, to send police and troops from outside forces to areas of possible disturbance in order to minimise the risk of sympathy and possible disaffection. In fact, the drafting of

'foreign' police and troops into the close-knit mining communities invariably exacerbated the situation leading to clashes that might otherwise have been avoided. However, titled and wealthy mineowners, who were often also local magistrates, were concerned only with the protection of their property and had no compunction in using their power and influence to send for troops and police on the least pretext. At Featherstone, a small mining town near Barnsley in the West Riding of Yorkshire, the hasty despatch of a telegram by Lord St. Oswald, a mineowner and magistrate, to the military commander in York was to result in the first killing of workers in Britain by British troops since the days of the Chartists, 'the Peterloo of the wage slaves' as it was called in a SDF pamphlet. A captain and fifty-three men were despatched to Wakefield, twenty-eight proceeding onwards to Featherstone. The arrival of the well-dressed, well-fed troops, tramping in columns over the cobbled streets of the little mining town aroused both curiosity and anger among the pinch-faced hungry miners and their families. The armed troops moved steadily to Akton Hall Colliery where they were later to bayonet charge the indignant and protesting miners and eventually, in the face of stone throwing, to open fire into the thickest portion of the crowd. Two men were killed and sixteen injured as the 'Featherstone Massacre' was blasted into the already bloody pages of the history of miners and mining. The combined strength of class privilege and state power is easily discerned in the photograph of cavalry (p.48) quartered at the palatial Wentworth Woodhouse, home of William Fitzwilliam, Earl of Stafford, who was keen to do his bit in forcing down the already abysmal wages of Britain's miners. The photograph of the West Riding Police (p.23), found on a council rubbish tip at Wakefield by a retired miner, shows the police wearing cutlasses while on duty at Houghton Main Colliery, further evidence of the forceful attitude of the authorities towards the strikers.

While police and cavalry were photographed for posterity there was little concern with leaving images of the poor. The observation of poverty towards the end of the nineteenth century is well documented by social explorers but rarely illustrated by the camera. The poor have left us no self record, for the camera was beyond their reach and social historians are left to regret that neither Charles Booth nor Jack London carried a Thornton Pickard or a Lancaster as they made their separate journeys into the abyss. While some photographers found street traders of pictorial interest and the closes of old Glasgow an architectural curiosity, there was little attempt to go into the homes and sweatshops to photograph the scenes so faithfully described by social investigators and socialist agitators. Some of the most compelling poverty photographs that survive were taken for religious and charitable organisations concerned with saving and helping children.

The photograph taken of a Ragged School (p.52) shows not only ragged clothes, but thin rickety legs, bare feet and the hollow-eyed accusative stare of children robbed of childhood. If Barnado was guilty at times of exaggerating the condition of his 'street arabs' while they were under the eye of the photographer, substantive pictures from the Church of England Children's Society, the Methodist Mission, and the Salvation Army confirm that the appearance of the children matches the descriptions left us by Sims, Sherhard and others. The photographs of children queuing for, and enjoying, farthing breakfasts (pp. 54,55) taken for the Salvation Army are a reminder of the tens of thousands of children who went to school hungry. The breakfasts provided by the slum sisters of the Army, a cup of hot tea and a jam butty, provided not only the best meal of the day but, to some, the only meal. These pictures were taken in the 1890s, but Lieutenant Colonel Cyril J. Barnes recalls that as late as 1935 he was serving farthing teas at Maerdy to the hungry children of Wales.

The photographs of children in a school playground and street (pp. 62,63) are memorials to the working class children who went to school barefoot. Robert Sherhard's description of the little milk carrier in Glasgow, a girl of ten years, whose 'feet felt and looked like pieces of frozen meat' drives away any illusions of the romance of going without shoes in the British climate. Barefoot children were a phenomenon that was not finally to leave us until the outbreak of the Second World War. For fifty years clog clubs and boot clubs flourished as parents scrimped and scraped to see their children shod and even then waged an endless struggle to keep boots and shoes in repair. In wet and wintry weather, rain and snow squelched through holes stuffed with brown paper as children shuffled to school, their footwear too large or too small, cast-offs from brothers and sisters. School for thousands came only after work, either casual help to local tradesmen or part-time work in factories and mills. The brittle yellowed photograph sent by Mrs Healey of the Wythernshaw Labour Party of cotton spinners at Millbrook near Oldham in the 1890s (p.53) shows the front row of operatives made up of half-timers. Legally allowed to start work at eleven years of age the children would clock on at five in the morning, working barefoot in the shattering noise and humid atmosphere of the mill before going exhausted to school in the afternoon. Health and education suffered but mill owners fought fiercely against attempts to deprive them of their cheap labour and it was not until the Education Act of 1918 that half-time work for children was legally ended.

While children were allowed to work part time, there were many adults for whom there was no work at all, or work that was seasonal or casual in the extreme. London alone had four hundred thousand casual workers in the 1890s and thousands were unemployed, homeless and destitute, a submerged population of outcasts who not only filled the workhouses and doss houses but slept in great numbers in the streets. Two of the SDF lantern slides show differing aspects of homelessness, a picture of women spending the night on an embankment seat, the photograph taken at four in the morning (p.59) and a scene of men washing themselves in a night shelter (p.61). Another remarkable picture taken inside a night shelter showing the bizarre and spartan sleeping arrangements has come from the archives of the Salvation Army. The men lay in boxes set on the floor, looking like rows of coffins, those in sleep resembling the dead and those awakening rising as in resurrection. The scene of women sleeping on the embankment seats would have been a common sight at the time. Drawings from *The Illustrated London News* of 1887 depict not only women, but women with babies in arms on the embankment seats at night. Trafalgar Square also had its nightly quota of open-air sleepers who each morning performed their ablutions in the famous fountains. This sight so annoyed the Vestry of St. Martin's-in-the-Fields that they complained to the Commissioner of Police about the people 'infesting the

place'. A night count, taken on 26 October 1887, showed four hundred homeless huddled together in the Square and the manager of the Oxford Music Hall described the spectacle as 'the most terrible sight of open-air human misery in Europe'.

The authorities were disturbed and the middle class afraid when the SDF began to organise the unemployed who assembled in the Square under the banner 'Not charity but work'. The memories of 8 February 1887, when the SDF lost control of a march of unemployed from the Square to Hyde Park and the windows of the rich men's clubs in Pall Mall had been smashed, were fresh enough for them to be fearful of the mob. On 17 October the Square was temporarily closed on the orders of Sir Charles Warren, Commissioner of Police, and the harassment of the unemployed and SDF meetings began in earnest. On 8 November a notice was posted banning all meetings in the Square and the arena was ready for massive confrontation. Outraged by the denial of free speech and assembly, a number of radical organisations called for a demonstration of protest on 13 November, a day to become known in the labour movement as Bloody Sunday. While the marchers assembled at various points in the capital, the Square was sealed off by two thousand five hundred police on foot, sixty mounted on horseback and supported by two hundred mounted troops of the 1st Life Guards, one hundred and fifty of the 2nd Life Guards and a detachment of the Grenadier Guards armed with rifles and fixed bayonets. In the ensuing mêlée, the Riot Act was read, two people were killed and at least two hundred demonstrators treated for injuries sustained by flailing batons and pounding hooves. William Morris and George Bernard Shaw witnessed the battle, Shaw admitting that he ran away, John Burns was arrested and Cunninghame Graham beaten and arrested. The following Sunday, following a protest rally in Hyde Park, the demonstrators made their way back to Trafalgar Square where the police, still present in large numbers charged the crowd again and a young workman, Alfred Linnell, was ridden down and subsequently died.

The agitation for 'Work, not charity' continued relentlessly over the years, the SDF leading the unemployed on regular sorties into the heart of Mayfair. The photograph of Westminster unemployed (p.79), printed from a SDF lantern slide, gives a vivid picture of the strength of the demonstrators as they invaded Berkeley Square in November 1905. 'Curse your charity, we want work' was the theme as the SDF with trade union support swept towards the homes of the wealthy. Twenty thousand roared approval at a Hyde Park rally after the incursion; as Jack Williams said 'you have starved too long. . . . .come out and parade the West End every day.' Williams was himself born to poverty and had escaped from the workhouse at the age of ten, climbing the walls of the Hornsey Union to freedom. He led the workless to the very doors of the rich, marching them on one occasion down Bond Street as policemen stood purposefully with their backs to the jewellers' windows. On another invasion day, to Belgrave Square, consternation was caused as a carpet of red baize laid across the pavement for a society wedding was torn to shreds by the marching boots of the unemployed.

Earlier in the year, London had seen the arrival of a column of trade unionists who had marched from Northamptonshire (pp. 74, 75). They came from Raunds, members of the National Union of Boot and Shoe Operatives, going in body to the War Office to protest against the cheap labour policy of the department in purchasing service boots at prices below an agreed tariff. The organiser of the march was James Gribble, a prominent member of the SDF, who had worked in the boot and shoe trade since he was twelve years old. A series of postcards commemorate the route march from Raunds to London, one card being dedicated to an unofficial hero of the protest, John Pearson (p.56). Gribble organised the march on military lines, selecting only the fittest men from hundreds of volunteers and appointing three 'officers' to take command of his men who were divided into six companies. With bicycle outriders and a horse-drawn ambulance, General Gribble, as he was dubbed, took no risks of his army falling by the wayside. Pearson, a crippled shoemaker, was determined to take part in the protest despite his infirmity. Forbidden to join the official march he swung his way to London on his crutches a few hundred yards ahead of Gribble's army, a lone but true hero of labour.

Another procession to London to be commemorated by a series of postcards was the march of four hundred unemployed from Leicester in 1905, representing two thousand men and their families (p.76). Negatives of the original cards were sent to Leicester Museum by an old socialist, Robert Barnes, who photographed the originals while they were in the possession of Charles White, son of the organising secretary of the march, George ('Sticky') White. Again the protest was planned on army lines, the men wearing their medals, carrying water bottles and blankets and marching in columns. The photograph of the men leaving the city, to the tune of 'Lead Kindly Light' was taken, according to Barnes, from the top of a stationary tram. Although well disciplined and selected from over eight hundred applicants for the trek, the men were in poor shape, suffering from months of being underfed, were badly shod and had only the scantiest of funds. At Market Harborough (p.77) they washed in troughs at the cattle market and slept in the cattle sheds. The journey was arduous and miserable, the men trampling through driving continuous rain, shoes leaking, making topcoats of sacks and living on bread, cheese and cocoa. Along the way, they learned that their request to see the King had been refused and it was a tired, ragged and soddened army that was given shelter and a meat tea by the Salvation Army at Edgware and asked by Ramsay McDonald to sign the pledge!

An unusual postcard is that depicting the SDF agitator Ernest Marklew (p.80) dressed in broad-arrowed prison clothes, published in 1906. The card is one of a small collection of socialist commemorative cards that belonged to Leonard Wood Wilkinson, a pioneer member of the Independent Labour Party. It is a reminder of the long years of struggle by early socialists to establish the right of free speech in public places. Since 1885, with the famous Dodd Street arrests in Limehouse, the SDF had been harassed by police while holding meetings at open-air pitches. Heavy fines and imprisonment with hard labour were imposed by middle class magistrates on socialists accused of obstruction and refusal to pay fines. At Nelson, as in London and other cities, socialists persisted in speaking at regular pitches despite repeated persecution. As one speaker was arrested, another would take his place and thousands came every Sunday, some from curiosity, some to give support, as the police fought their way through crowds to drag away speaker after speaker. The secretary of the Nelson branch of the SDF, Bryan Chapman, was also imprisoned during the free speech fight at Nelson, but no photograph has been found to accompany the oakum-picking portrait of his comrade, Ernest Marklew.

In 1908, the unemployed in Manchester tried a new tactic in drawing public attention to their plight. Following a meeting of about five hundred out of work men, they were urged to march on Manchester Cathedral by a man named Freewood. Arriving during the litany, they were turned away by the warden but told to come back in the afternoon. The photograph (p.81) shows the amazing sight of the unemployed men, now some fifteen hundred strong, pouring into the cathedral, watched by smartly dressed middle class onlookers. The origin of the picture, now in Manchester City Library, is unknown but an account of the uproar caused by a sermon preached by the vicar of Rochdale indicates the desperate position of the hungry men. Asking for food and clothing, the vicar promised sympathy only and as men rose to the clatter of falling prayer books to interrupt, the Dean had to declare the service over. At a meeting after the service Freewood read a prayer that he had tried to read in the cathedral, ending 'O Lord we beseech thee to move thy servant Bishop Knox (Archbishop of Canterbury) to see that something more than sympathy is needed and that his influence brought to bear on our Parliament might bear some fruit.'

The rising militancy of the trade unions and the determination of the government to meet that militancy with armed force if necessary is shown in two photographs taken during 1911 of incidents from the transport strike at Liverpool and the first national railway stoppage. From Liverpool, where gun boats were sent up the Mersey to train their guns on Birkenhead and cavalry and infantry were drafted, comes a powerful study of a docker exchanging verbal blows with an army sergeant while a platoon of astonished infantrymen with fixed bayonets regard with the awe the audacity of the worker (p.91). The railway photograph (p.92) from the Library of the National Railway Museum shows armed guardsmen and police on duty at the Clapham Junction North signal box. Tom Mann answered the drafting of troops to Liverpool by saying 'Let Churchill do his utmost, his best or his worst, let him order ten times more military to Liverpool, not all the King's horses and all the King's men can take the vessels out of the docks to sea.' The Liverpool strikers won their battle as did the rail strikers.

The success of the dockers and railmen seems to have inspired a revolt of women workers in the area of London's dockland. A photograph of distribution of loaves of bread, believed to have been taken outside the Labour Institute, Fort Road, Bermondsey, survives as a relic of an uprising of the unorganised (p.93). Women and girls walked out of jam, biscuit and pickle factories and marched around Bermondsey calling on other women in the food factories to join them in claiming an increase on their incredibly low wages. Out came the women and girls from the factories with household names, Spillers, Pearce Duffs, Hartley's, Pink's and Lipton's, where they worked for as little as seven shillings a week. Laughing, singing, welcoming the escape from the hot and stifling factories they revelled in an August heatwave as they paraded the streets. The trade unions and labour movement responded to their call, Ben Tillett, Mary MacArthur, Herbert Burrows and Dr Salter addressing fifteen thousand of the strikers in Southwark Park. In three weeks, increases had been won at eighteen of the twenty-one factories where the women had struck.

Two photographs taken in 1914 at South Shields (pp. 94,95) mark another revolt of unorganised and exploited women, this time in the herring industry. The women worked at gutting herrings, stinking work carried out at a frenetic pace with razor sharp knives, earning threepence an hour for an average working week of sixty-four hours. The industry was small, but highly profitable for the owners who exported the salted and cured herrings to Eastern Europe, making so much money that they referred to the trade among themselves as 'Klondyking'. The strike began with a spontaneous walk-out of women from factories in North Shields and quickly spread across the Tyne to South Shields, the women asking for sixpence an hour and payment for overtime. The women were enthusiastically supported by James Wilson of the National Amalgamated Union of Labour but seemed to have appointed their own leaders and to have enjoyed asserting their independence. The photographs included in this collection, and two others that survive, show only women present during incidents in the strike. The photograph of women drinking in the street is particularly intriguing, for even in the Mile End Road, one of the toughest port-side streets in Shields, this would have been an unusual sight. It would seem that the women were openly expressing their defiance of the system that robbed them and treated them as inferior. The strike was never won or lost, for with the declaration of war on 4 August 1914, the herring fleet was commandeered by the Royal Navy for the duration of the war.

For socialists, the war was a negation of internationalism, splitting the movement as workers from one land hastened to shoot down the workers of another. On 2 August 1914, just two days before the declaration of war, a huge anti-war meeting was held in Trafalgar Square. Called by the British section of the International Socialist Bureau, a manifesto, whose signatories included Keir Hardie and Arthur Henderson, was read to the gathering, it ended with the words, 'down with class rule, down with the rule of brute force, down with war, up with the peaceful rule of the people.' Speakers included J. Stokes, Chairman of the London Trades Council, Will Thorne, Mary MacArthur, Margaret Bondfield, Herbert Burrows and Keir Hardie. That was 2 August. By 5 August the Labour Party supported the war. H. G. Wells proclaimed the sword had been drawn for peace. Massingham, the radical journalist recanted in *The Daily News* the opposition to the war he had proclaimed in *The Nation* the previous week. Labour and trade union leaders joined in recruiting campaigns and Will Thorne who had declared against the war at the Trafalgar Square rally became a Lieutenant Colonel in the West Ham Volunteers.

Workers enlisted in their hundreds of thousands and it was left to the pacifist section of the labour movement together with a handful of true internationalists to preserve the socialist conscience. The ILP published an anti-war manifesto that declared 'Out of the darkness and the depth we hail our working class comrades of every land. Across

WEST RIDING POLICE ON DUTY AT HOUGHTON MAIN COLLIERY. DURING STRIKE. OCT. 8th, 1893.

the roar of guns we send sympathy and greetings to the German socialists. . . .' It was truly a cry out of darkness for the wall posters in the recruiting photograph (p.99), 'It's our flag' and 'Take up the sword of justice', evoke the jingoism of the times.

The war opened industry to women and there is no shortage of propaganda-style photographs to show women at 'unlady-like' work, cleaning railway engines, filling shells, humping parcels and wearing every sort of uniform from the livery of Salford gas meter inspectors to London bus conductors. The two photographs of women at war-time work (pp. 100,101) are both of an official nature but do represent women at the kind of heavy industrial work that would not have been readily open to them before the outbreak of the war.

As the generals demanded more and more young men for the muddy walk to mutilation and death on the Western Front, so the opportunities for women to replace them in their jobs at home grew. Of course there were problems and a degree of resistance especially from male workers in skilled industries such as engineering. The Amalgamated Society of Engineers, an all-male union with a long tradition of craft skill, saw the introduction of lower paid unskilled labour as a threat to post-war job security. The official policy of the government of 'dilution of labour' which led to the scrapping of apprenticeship agreements, increasing working hours and the speeding up of production deepened those fears. The doubts of trade unionists about the large scale introduction of female labour into industry were expressed in a composite resolution at the 1915 Trades Union Congress from the Scientific Instrument Makers and the Provincial Association of Operative Cotton Spinners of Bolton asking for committees to be set up to ensure 'the replacement of women at the close of the war by more suitable male labour'. The real threat, however, was the inequality of pay between men and women and to their credit, many trade union leaders insisted on equal pay for women doing equal work, achieving a limited success. Unions recruited the new women workers and by 1918 membership of unions affiliated to the TUC had risen by well over two million from the outbreak of war.

The photographs sent to me for the era between the world wars are dominated by unemployment and strife. The pictures have the smell of poverty, mean, grinding and unrelenting, and the stories that accompany them are of petty oppression and soulless stinginess on the part of the people with power, the rich, governments and their paid officials. The photograph of the eviction of an agricultural worker and his family (p.108) mocks the 'homes for heroes' slogan of Lloyd George and the picture of unemployed ex-servicemen (p.109) is a mirror of broken promises. The pictures of girl domestic servants (pp. 106,107) recall the story of Alice Pattinson, a chronicle of the meanness of the well off and the utter poverty of the poor. Here was a child of fourteen years with no hope of finding work in her home town on Tyneside because of severe unemployment. Alone, she was sent by coach to London to become a servant to a family selected from a sixpenny agency. The young girl was made to rise at five each morning, her first job being to pump up water in readiness for the family to bath. Three hundred pumps. There followed a catalogue of scivvying, ending at eleven at night after pumping the water again before retreating to her box-room

to cry herself to sleep. Her pay was ten shillings a week and the parsimony of her employer demanded the deduction of one shilling a week until she had paid twenty-eight shillings, the cost of her coach ticket to London. A further burden dictated by their stinginess meant that Alice had to pay for her own uniforms, sending precious shillings each week to the clothing club. From the balance of her meagre wages, Alice sent home money each week to her mother to help feed her younger brothers and sisters. It was three years before the lonely girl saved enough money to return home to visit her family. The sheer helplessness of the girl and the agony of her parents are not difficult to imagine, but the tale of Alice was but a single episode arising from the devastating effect of unemployment on family life and was repeated in endless variety among millions of families.

An example of petty oppression is commemorated on a postcard issued by the Park and Dare Lodge of the South Wales Miners' Federation in 1920 to mark an act of heartless indifference by the Ocean Coal Company towards their workers. Wanting to attend the funeral of a good comrade, the men asked permission to leave work one hour early, offering to make up the time by starting the shift one hour sooner than usual. The management bluntly refused and the miners were forced to go to the funeral of their comrade in their pit clothes, straight from work. In the tradition of the Cherhill eviction carte-de-visite, the union commissioned a local photographer to record the shameful event as evidence of the unfeeling and inflexible attitude of the mineowners. The postcard has been kept over the years by G. L. Clarke, a former miner, as a keepsake of the 'good old days.'

By contrast with the impenitent mineowners, the photograph from Ashington (p.112) pictures the compassion of mineworkers for their less fortunate brothers and sisters. Taken in December 1922, the photograph records the distribution of money to aged miners and widows to bring some comfort for Christmas. The care and concern shown by the Ashington miners was at a time when they were still suffering financial hardship as a result of the 1921 lock-out.

The smell of poverty wafts from the photograph of Ernest Bevin preparing a 'docker's breakfast' (p.113) as evidence for the Shaw inquiry of 1920. The potatoes are peeled into a chipped enamel bowl, while the little girl watching is seen wearing boots that must surely have come from her brother. Bevin, national organiser of the Dockers' Union, used his own experience of poverty and his deep knowledge and feeling for the dock workers in presenting the case for decasualisation and higher wages. Faced with the expert evidence for the employers as to the precise number of calories on which a docker could live and work, Bevin went shopping in Canning Town and prepared a breakfast from the appropriate proportion of the weekly wage. In the court, Bevin pushed the scraps of bacon, bread and fish before the Cambridge professor giving evidence on nutrition. Was that enough for a man who had to carry 2 cwt. sacks on his back all day, he asked? Had the professor ever spent eight hours carrying 2 cwt. sacks? He then flourished a menu from the Savoy Hotel and asked the professor to calculate the number of calories in a shipowner's lunch!

The photographs that precede the pictures of the General Strike, and lock-out of 1926, are a backdrop for the struggle that follows. The images are of heavy wet pit clothes drying in front of a kitchen range (p.118), a miner kneeling at a zinc bath while his wife pours in a bowl of hot water (p.119), a boy working underground with his pit pony (p.120), and a scene of northern mining life (p.121) where a local agitator harangues his audience, men with clogs, caps and pigeon baskets. The pictures create an impression of mining life but they cannot convey the horrific danger of the work, for even the statistics elude the experience. Every five hours a miner was killed. Every ten minutes, five maimed. In three years from 1922 to 1924, more than half a million were injured badly enough to be off work for seven days or more. The reward for the daily risk to health and life varied from eight shillings and five pence a day to ten shillings and nine pence a day according to district. That was the wage the owners insisted on cutting. That was the toil the owners insisted on lengthening. The Duke of Hamilton drew royalties of more than £100,000 a year from the hacking, backbreaking, sweating labour of the miners beneath 'his' earth. Owners included wealthy aristocrats like Lord Londonderry and the Duke of Northumberland. Supporting the owners was a reactionary Conservative government that included Churchill, Hicks and Chamberlain.

Most of the photographs sent by trade unionists do not cover the period of the strike itself but show aspects of the long lone fight of the miners to survive the lock-out. Pictures of soup kitchens came from almost every coal field as did photographs of miners in fancy dress for fund-raising days. The main impression in sifting photographs of the event was the sharp class division between strikers and government supporters. Compare the children and women in the photograph of the soup kitchen queue at Rotherham (p.124) with the swaggering polo-playing 'specials' (p.127). Contrast the well-fed troops carrying ammunition into the Tower of London (p.126) with the miners at Cheadle, scratching for fuel (p.130). Press photographs of volunteers who engaged in strike-breaking activities show them wearing plus-fours, cricket pullovers and blazers, the specials in similar attire but with the addition of tin hats, blue and white police armbands and truncheons which they waved for every photographer. For the miners it was a fight for survival, for the middle class dads and their strike-breaking undergraduate sons it was all jolly good fun. *The Times* and the Great Western Railway handed out silver ashtrays as souvenirs to strike breakers and Baldwin and Hicks signed 'thank you' certificates by the thousand. The boys of Westminster School who helped pack the strike edition of *The Times* were each presented with a silver matchbox bearing *The Times* crest and the Latin motto *Ictus meus utilus esto* freely translated as 'may my strike be of some use.' All very amusing for 'top people' and public school boys who shared the joke while miners were engaged in a daily battle to find bread for their children (p.131).

The decision to strike in support of the miners followed the posting of lock-out notices at the pit heads on 16 April 1926 by the mineowners and the expiry of the deadline for the acceptance of their new and adverse terms on 30 April. At the special conference of trade union executives at the Memorial Hall, Farringdon Road, London, on 1 May, Bevin in a committed and passionate speech said of the decision to strike in defence of the miners '. . . . . if every penny goes, if every asset goes, history will ultimately write up that it was a magnificent generation that was prepared to do it rather than see the miners driven down like slaves.'

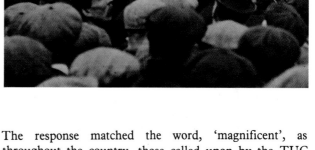

The response matched the word, 'magnificent', as throughout the country, those called upon by the TUC to stop work did so with enthusiasm and solidarity.

The photograph of building workers marching in support of the miners (p.122) was a response repeated in a thousand towns. Meetings were held, trade union news sheets printed daily, committees set up to control the movement of supplies, organise pickets (Bolton organised 2,280 pickets in two days), provide entertainment and supply speakers to put the argument for standing firm with the miners. At the height of the strike, with messages of support pouring into the TUC, the number of strikers growing and spirits high, the TUC called off the strike. The reasoning behind the decision has been argued ever since, but the owners and the Conservatives had no doubt whatsoever that it was an unconditional surrender. The miners refused to accept the cut in wages and increase in hours demanded by the owners and the government, and remained locked out for six months until driven back by starvation and impending winter.

There are photographs that recall the ingenuity of miners in scraping together the bare necessities for survival (pp. 130,133) but none that record the misery of the victimisation that followed the ending of the strike. Courageous men in lonely country districts who had struck in twos and threes were easy victims for retribution. On the railways, men with years of loyal service were demoted, moved to posts far from home or simply not re-engaged and the NUR was forced to sign a humiliating document that included the words 'the trade unions admit that in calling a strike they committed a wrongful act.' The words of Ernest Bevin spoken at the end of the strike, 'Thousands will be victimised as a result of this day's work', were prophetically true. as employers declared open shop and sacked those who argued. The Conservative government revelled in the defeat of the strike and turned to the slow crushing of the miners. They sent an official note of protest to the Soviet government in an effort to stop the collection of relief money by Russian trade unionists. Chamberlain instructed the authorities to tighten up on relief payments which were already at a starvation figure of five shillings for a wife and two shillings for each child. The men were precluded from Poor Relief by a law originating from a court action brought by the Powell Duffryn Steam Coal Company in 1898. Lord Askwith urged the cessation of all relief payments. When, after months of hunger and deprivation, the miners organised a fund raising mission to the United States, Baldwin wrote to the US authorities to say there was 'no dire need in the coalfields'. This at a time when Will John, MP for Rhondda West, was telling the Board of Guardians that women were now carrying their children to the communal kitchens because the children had no shoes. Four million British citizens were put on the rack of hunger by a Cabinet of rich men.

The employers final reckoning came with the slow return to work at the end of the year. The owners prepared blacklists and gave them to the police at the pit heads. Some men never worked again until 1939. The memory became seared into the culture and folklore of mining communities and W. P. Richardson of the Durham miners expressed the feelings of his people when he said 'The miners are on the bottom and have been compelled to accept dictated and unjust terms. The miners will rise again and will remember because they cannot forget. The victors of today will live to regret their unjust treatment of the miners.'

Three rarely seen photographs from three consecutive years at the end of the 1920s recall the broad range of left wing activity at that time. From 1927, John Bull, a member of the Electrical Trades Union for fifty years, sent a precious remembrance of the campaign in Britain to save the lives of two Italian immigrants in the United States, Sacco and Vanzetti (p.135). The dated picture with Overland car and orator with giant megaphone holds a fragmentary moment in the attempt by world-wide progressive movements to obtain clemency for the two poor anarchists who were convicted amid an atmosphere of hysteria and hatred against radicals. Twenty thousand answered the call to the rally in Hyde Park advertised on the banner in the picture, and John Bull tells of the baton charges by the police to disperse the crowd that had gathered to hear George Hicks (Chairman of the TUC), Wal Hannington and A. J. Cook, denounce the sentence.

From Elsie Parker, a pioneer member of the Communist Party came a rare view of a procession of the Women's Red Army, marching through the East End of London to manoeuvres in Epping Forest in 1928 (p.138). The marchers, overtly the women's section of the Labour League of Ex-servicemen, are seen wearing uniforms described as consisting of serviceable short skirt, fawn coloured blouse, khaki beret, flat heeled walking shoes, regulation armband and red tie. Apparently modelled on the German Red Front Fighters, the women who were accused by the Commissioner of Police of performing military movements in the forest, succeeded in persuading him that they were only practising their marching in readiness for May Day!

Helen Hathaway of the Reading North Labour Party contributed a splendid picture of women supporters of *The Daily Herald* at the start of a circulation campaign inspired by the election of the 1928 Labour government. 'Labour has arrived' proclaimed the poster proudly held by the working class women lined up for the photograph. Few could have foreseen how soon and how treacherously it was to depart. The desertion of McDonald, Snowden and Thomas from the cause they had espoused for so many years ripped through the movement and reduced the number of Labour members in Parliament from 289 to 46. 'Every Duchess in Britain will want to kiss me tonight' said Ramsay McDonald on becoming Prime Minister of the National Government. The yellowed print from the walls of Transport House (p.142) shows the Transport and General Workers' Union secretary, Ernest Bevin, at Gateshead in 1931, with a band of loyal Labour Party supporters. 'Abolish poverty, abolish slums, wipe out destitution' reads the poster on the election van. It was Bevin that was to be wiped out from the parliamentary scene, losing a safe Labour seat to the National Liberal candidate by 12,938 votes.

The Snowden proposal to effect economies by cutting maintenance for the unemployed was to precipitate the biggest and most controversial demonstrations witnessed in Britain, the hunger marches of the 1930s. Ellen Wilkinson, Labour Member of Parliament for Jarrow and organiser of the 1936 Jarrow Crusade was to write 'The poverty of the poor is not an accident, a temporary difficulty, a personal fault. It is the permanent state in which the vast majority of the citizens of any capitalist country have to live. This is a basic fact of the class struggle, which not all the well meant efforts of Personal Service Leagues and Social Service Councils can gloss over.' The magnitude of the statement is perhaps only fully appreciated by a generation who are now old age pensioners, the working class men and women of adult age who lived through the torture of persistent unemployment, low wages, the means test and calculated class repression.

The fight back against the means test policy of the National Government was swiftly and efficiently organised. The first photograph of the hundreds sent in as snapshot jolts to the memory of those dreadful years came from Bill McQuilkin, a former District Secretary of the Amalgamated Engineering Union and forty years a member of the Paisley and District Trades Council. It shows Wal Hannington, organiser of the National Unemployed Workers' Movement, together with Harry McShane, leader of the Scottish unemployed, heading a Scots contingent on the march to London in October 1932. Skilfully organised by the NUWM, representative groups of unemployed workers set off from various regions of Britain to link up for a united entry to the capital city. They bore with them a petition signed by more than a million people which they planned to present to Parliament. The petition voiced four demands, the first of which was for the abolition of the means test. Under the new system a person who was unemployed for twenty-six weeks in a year was removed from statutory benefit and became a transitional claimant under the jurisdiction of the Public Assistance Committee. The family of the unemployed person was then assessed as to their needs based on the Poor Law relief scales of roughly ten shillings a week for an adult and three shillings a week for a child. The amount by which the income of the family exceeded the relief scales was then deducted from the benefit of the claimant. If it exceeded the relief scale then the unemployed claimant could be disqualified from benefit and his maintenance made the responsibility of the household. The effect on family life was devastating. A young boy or girl of fourteen years of age, starting a first job, could find him or herself responsible for contributing to the maintenance of an unemployed father, brother or sister. It was a policy of making the poor keep the poor, removing the financial burden of unemployment from the state to the family. Tens of thousands of cases of hardship were reported to the TUC as means test officers brutally enforced the system of household assessment. To quote one example from Newcastle, a single man, unemployed, was living with his married sister and her husband. The sister had no income but her unemployed brother was disallowed benefit because her husband was working. In vain did the husband protest that he could not be responsible for keeping his wife's brother.

The means test became synonymous with poverty and humiliation as government investigators pried into the personal finances of family life. War disability pensions, old age, widows' and orphans' pensions, trade union benefits, post office or Co-op savings, all had to be divulged so that family resources could be assessed. Len Willis, a printer from north London recalled that his unemployed father had an old and broken accumulator wireless set given to him by a friend. He repaired the set and when the means test officer called at the house the father was told that he could sell his wireless set if he needed money! Any employed member of a household was liable to interrogation in the zealous application of economy measures by government officials and even neighbours were approached in the quest for information about the financial status of a claimant. The TUC presented a memorandum to the Minister of Labour in 1932, strongly condemning the excesses of investigating officers. The memorandum ended, 'The General Council of the Trade Union Congress are confident that they are expressing the view of the majority of the country when they say that the public never intended and would not tolerate for an instant, the harassing and persecution of the unfortunate unemployed.'

The other demands of the 1932 hunger marchers—for the restoration of the ten per cent cut in benefit, the abolition of the Anomalies Act, the restoration of cuts in the social services as well as the abolition of the hated means test—were campaigned for in every city. As the winter approached there were demonstrations close to riots as hungry men stormed town halls and Public Assistance Committee offices demanding work or adequate maintenance. Tens of thousands demonstrated in West Ham, North Shields, Glasgow, Liverpool, Birkenhead and even in suburban Croydon. Well meaning social and charitable organisations tried hard to keep the unemployed off the streets, provide them with something useful to do and incidentally discourage participation in militant protest. The picture of unemployed making rope mats (p.146), sent by Chris Makepeace, a NALGO member from Cheshire, is a good example, the photograph being taken in the Bootle Services Club and the activity organised by local Rotarians and businessmen.

From the collection of Maud Brown, Women's Organiser of the NUWM, came copies of a series of photographs covering the hunger marches of 1934 and 1936. Maud Brown herself took part in the marches and was an indefatigable champion of the jobless and the poor. On one occasion, during a tenants' protest at a council meeting in Aberdeen, she hurled a live rat, taken from a slum dwelling at the assembled councillors. The pictures of the 1934 march (pp. 148-151) were taken of the women's column which marched to London from Derby. From the inscriptions on the back of the photographs, they were evidently intended for use in a French newspaper or magazine. The pictures capture the feeling of comradeship and purpose that existed between the marchers on their wintry trek to London. The shots of hay-box heated food being served by the roadside and the first aid treatment to blistered feet demonstrate the determination of the women not to starve in silence. All the marchers were unemployed or had out-of-work husbands and depended on the goodwill of local labour organisations to provide nightly accommodation during the journey. Hospitality from a Cooperative society in providing a meal with unaccustomed waiter service (p.149) is depicted in a scene that strikes a

balance between frugality and luxury. The chef is wearing the traditional tall hat as tea, bread and butter and pies are served in chilling surroundings.

An act of unbelievable parsimony is recalled by the photograph of unemployed workers at Stockport (p.152) in a placard parade against the decision of the council to spend three thousand pounds on royal jubilee celebrations while people went hungry. The protest led by the Stockport Labour Party did prod the Conservative council into issuing a half-crown voucher to the unemployed to mark the royal event. However, so deeply ingrained was the habit of keeping fists tightly clenched on the ratepayers' money when it came to dealing with the poor that the council excluded any old age pensioners in receipt of public assistance! To match their loyal meanness, the mill owners gave their workers a one day holiday so that they could join in the jubilation, and stopped them one day's pay!

If the means test was synonymous with poverty, then poverty was synonymous with South Wales. In Merthyr in 1936, unemployment was almost sixty per cent, and more than seventy per cent of the unemployed were subjected to the means test. Clothes were threadbare, boots a luxury, soup kitchens a necessity and prosperity a fantasy. The NUWM had no difficulty in raising a Welsh contingent of eight hundred men for the biggest and most united of the hunger marches against the means test in November 1936. Two postcard size photographs, personal souvenirs of that colossal protest, came from South Wales (p.155). The first, already described, was from Amos Mouls, the other, from Trevor Roberts, at that time an unemployed miner who marched with the Mountain Ash column and is seen standing immediately next to the banner from the Aberdare valley, being a portrait of Keir Hardie and emblazoned, '1936, poverty amidst plenty'. The group photograph, taken at Abereynon station as the marchers prepared to take the train to the assembly point at Cardiff, includes officials from the Aberdare and Mountain Ash trades councils, local Labour councillors and the joint secretaries of the United Front Movement.

In London, a quarter of a million greeted the marchers at a huge demonstration in Hyde Park as contingents from all the depressed areas marched in, presenting themselves as emissaries of the millions suffering as victims of a rotten social system. Speakers from all sections of the labour movement were on the six platforms, including Attlee, Bevan and Hannington. 'The hunger marchers' said Bevan, 'have achieved one thing. They have for the first time in the history of the labour movement achieved a united platform. Communists, ILPers, Socialists, members of the Labour Party and Co-operators for the first time have joined hands together and we are not going to unclasp them.'

The years of popular left unity, of the Left Book Club, support for the Spanish Republic and the united fight against fascism at home and abroad are recalled by three photographs. A press picture from *The Daily Worker* (p.161) of a great united anti-fascist protest in Trafalgar Square, a snapshot from a woman Labour Party member of another anti-fascist gathering at Belle Vue, Manchester (p.166), and a press photograph from *Reynolds News* (p.167) of an aid for Spain section of the 1938 May Day demonstration in London. In the photograph taken in Trafalgar Square in 1937, Mosley and his followers are seen giving the Nazi salute, their demonstration ringed by a great phalanx of anti-fascists, their clenched fists raised in the salute of the United Front. Interestingly, despite the hatred each side nurtured for the other, a single line of foot policemen was all that separated the opponents and the protest passed without violence, Mosley's speech being drowned by the mass singing of The Internationale. The snapshot taken earlier in 1937, shows women Labour Party members of the New Cross Ward, Manchester, at another United Front anti-Mosley rally, this time at Belle Vue. Again, the protest passed without real violence as the supporters of the United Front rendered Mosley's speech inaudible to all except those in the front row as they sang The Red Flag and maintained a constant barrage of anti-fascist slogans. The picture of nurses collecting money for 'milk for Spain' at the 1938 May Day in London is a catalyst to the memory of the fervent support given by the left wing of the labour movement to the cause of the Spanish Republicanism, the cause for which so many of the finest workers and intellectuals of the movement literally gave their lives. The 1938 May Day rally in London was the largest since 1926 and the message of the day was 'Spain above all'.

The fight against unemployment in Britain continued throughout the winter of 1938-39, the NUWM changing their tactics from national hunger marches to a series of spectacular public stunts. Unemployed invaded the Ritz, chained themselves to railings, held an Unemployment Assistance Board officer prisoner in a labour exchange and stopped the traffic in Oxford Street by laying down in the road (p.168). The threat of war overshadowed domestic problems and in 1938-39 air raid shelters were being distributed, sandbags filled and thirty-eight million gas masks issued to the public. 'Mickey Mouse' was enlisted to help persuade reluctant children to wear the claustrophobic, rubber-smelling masks (p.169) and the photograph of the little girl together with her doll, wearing her Mickey Mouse gas mask is a horror picture that presaged the horror of war that was to descend on Britain and the world in 1939.

Photographs of the war period were taken by the million by official photographers but snapshot pictures by working people declined sharply for reasons of scarcity of film, processing facilities, restrictions and pre-occupation with the more serious business of involvement in the war. There was censorship of published photographs and the pictures of bomb damage (pp. 170,175) bear the rubber stamp mark 'passed by censor'. The immediate post-war period was severely affected by shortages and the after-effects of the massive conflict and it was to be some years before popular photography was restored as a normal chronicler of holidays, relatives, fun and work.

For the labour movement the war strengthened the commitment of 'no return to the thirties'. After the experience of fighting from Dunkirk to Berlin, and in deserts and jungles, there was a resolve to refuse to return to a Britain of class privilege, private wealth and public squalor. Churchill, so popular during the war (although his picture on the cinema screen in South Wales would still raise some boos and jeers) had nothing to offer the working class in peace. He could merely bluster a threat in an election broadcast on 4 June 1945, that a socialist government would bring 'some sort of Gestapo'. The people were not to be deceived and, in July 1945, elected the most widely representative and popular democratic government in British history. The Labour Party polled almost twelve million votes, winning 393 seats in a euphoria of social revolution. Men and women from elementary schools and secondary schools, miners, agricultural labourers, lorry drivers, engineers and clerks took their seats alongside their colleagues from the universities and the professions. The happiness at the result, evidenced in the photograph taken at Transport House (p.181) on the news of the victory, was echoed throughout the land. The long, long night was over; for old socialists this was the millennium. People openly wept with joy and the newly elected Labour members caught the spirit of the jubilation and the victory by singing The Red Flag in the House of Commons to the disbelief and demoralised bewilderment of the Conservatives.

With a clear cut mandate for radical social change, the Labour government embarked on a programme designed to alleviate the worst aspects of capitalism. In a country shattered by six years of war, with more than four million houses damaged or destroyed and widespread bomb damage to docks, railways and factories, the government faced an unprecedented task of reconstruction amid a world-wide shortage of food and building materials. Against such a background the Labour government established the National Health Service, raised the school leaving age, introduced compensation for injury at work, comprehensive social security, family allowances and nationalised electricity, gas, road haulage, the Bank of England, airlines, cable and wireless companies and the coal mines. In Durham, miners and their families danced in the streets at the 1947 Gala (p.184) hailing nationalisation as 'the dawn of a new era' and emblazoning their banners with portraits of their new heroes of labour, Attlee, Bevan, Dalton, Shinwell and Cripps.

That the old era had passed, few questioned as Labour legislated. Yet what of the spirit of socialism, the co-operative commonwealth of man? By 1947, it seemed that for too many Labour leaders the spirit of socialism appeared more as a ghost from the past to haunt them as a spectre. In 1948, the Home Secretary, Chuter Ede, banned the May Day march of the London Trades Council (p.186), the first time since the inaugural march in 1890 that trade unionists had been deprived of their right to take to the streets on labour's own day. In itself, the decision was not of great import, but one wonders what sort of socialist it was that allowed himself to be cornered into such an absurd decision as the result of the activities of a discredited fascist, the demagogue Mosley. The ghosts of Morris, Burns, Hyndman and a galaxy of pioneers for the Cause must have marched in silent protest on that day.

If the dream of a new and golden Jerusalem to be 'builded here' faded from the hearts of those elected as master builders, the hope yet remains with the many. The photographs in this book serve to remind us of the sacrifices made by those who cherished socialism as the hope of mankind, who believed in the brotherhood of organised labour and bequeathed us the labour movement as the foundation stone for the co-operative commonwealth, and not as a stepping stone to consumer capitalism.

The glass plate from which this print was taken was found at 444 Woolwich Road, Charlton, in 1965, shortly before the demolition of the premises. The men are limeburners and worked in conditions of extreme heat, the lime being produced by calcination in small kilns at a temperature of 898°C.

The business was owned by Frederick George Nichols in 1887 and he was probably the owner when his workers were photographed in the 1870s. In the 1920s, the business was acquired by the Crown Fuel Company who amalgamated them with their own works next door. Crown Fuel made gas fire elements and ceramics for industry and later diversified to producing pottery vases and animal figures for export, the works being known as the Greenwich Pottery.

This early picture of a group of joiners was taken at Carnoustie by J. S. Cameron. The top-hatted figure is presumably the owner, seated with his workmen to mark an unrecorded occasion. The men are wearing the traditional aprons of their craft and the tools they carry are easily recognisable. The boy in the straw hat holds a rebate plane, the owner a carpenter's rule, while two of the men in the back row hold hammers in readiness to strike the irons from jack plane and block plane.

Although an obviously small workshop, it is possible that the men may have been members of the Associated Carpenters and Joiners of Scotland, formed in 1861. By 1877, about the time the photograph was taken, the union membership had grown to 8,979 members. The union was more militant than its larger counterpart in England (the Amalgamated Society of Carpenters and Joiners). Friendly benefits were optional and there was a trade section contributing only for strike and unemployment pay.

In 1875, the rate for the job was sixpence an hour for a fifty-seven hour week and as skilled craftsmen, members considered themselves to be aristocrats of labour.

William Paterson, the secretary of the union who held office from 1868 until 1883, was appointed that year to be the first working class factory inspector in Scotland. The union made attempts to extend its influence beyond Scotland but was hampered by the name and in May 1887 dropped Scotland from the title. Eventually the union amalgamated with the English ASC & J in 1911.

'Dissent and unionism their only crime' was the caption to this photograph taken at Cherhill, Wiltshire, on 10 February 1876. Mr W. Durham, on the right, had dared to stand up to the tyranny of the local squire, G. H. W. Heneage and his relative, C. W. Heneage, who between them owned most of the village of Cherhill. The result was the eviction of Durham and his family from the cottage where he had lived for twenty-eight years. Discernible in the picture are two items among their few possessions which illustrate the nature of Durham's independence which so infuriated the feudal Heneages: a collecting box for the Wesleyan Missionary Society and a framed poster bearing a portrait of Joseph Arch, founder of the National Union of Agricultural Labourers.

The paternal squire used to administer a coal and clothing club, adding a little of his own money to the regular contributions of his farm labourers. For the privilege of the squire's modest contribution the farm labourers' wives would have their clothing inspected by Mrs Heneage in her drawing room and would receive a good scolding if they dared to purchase any garment 'beyond their station in life'. Each woman was asked 'is your husband in the union?' If they answered 'yes', they were not allowed to belong to the club.

When a new tenancy agreement was issued to the Heneage employees in 1875, two trade unionists, one of whom was Durham and a small tradesman who was a Liberal and friendly to the union, were given notice to quit. Forcible evictions were nothing new to the Heneages; when a widow refused to leave her cottage, they simply tore off the roof. Determined to stamp out support for Arch's union, Heneage evicted Mr and Mrs Durham, their two sons and twelve year old daughter, their goods and chattels being dumped in the field outside. The girl was also forbidden to attend the village school.

The following week, a meeting of protest was held near the village in a field loaned by a sympathiser, Mr John Clark. The meeting, supported by the NUAL and the *English Labourer*, was attended by a thousand farm workers, despite pouring rain and the risk of incurring retribution from the squire and his relations. They sang, 'When Arch Beneath The Wellesbourne Tree', chorus

> Though rich and great our cause may bare,
> We care not for their frown,
> The strongest are not strong enough,
> To keep the labourer down.

EVICTED AT CHERHILL, WILTS, FEB. 10 1876 BY C. W. HENEAGE ,ESQ., V.C., J.P.

By the 1880s, more than three hundred thousand men were employed in running the numerous private railways that were a central part of the industrial wealth of the nation. For the worker, the railways offered 'a steady job', they also conferred respectability, for a railway servant had to be sober, honest and reliable. For the prize of job security there was a price to be paid and the demands of the railway companies were stringent. Discipline was military in character and enforced by an elaborate system of fines and suspensions. Monthly punishment lists were published and posted and extracts from a London Brighton and South Coast Railway list reveal 'a porter suspended for three weeks for quarrelling with an outside porter', a porter discharged for intoxication, 'a hammerman fined for losing time' and 'a telegraph clerk fined for violently using his instrument'. Many railwaymen lived in company cottages and in those cases, dismissal would be accompanied by eviction.

Hours of work were arbitrarily decided by the railway companies and overtime was compulsory and paid at the ordinary rate. Most of the companies did not grant holidays, but where three days or so were allowed, they might depend, as they did on the Midland, upon a points system for general tidiness. Excessive hours of work were directly connected with safety and were to be key issues in the building of railway trade unionism. The attitude of the companies to trade unionism was one of mutiny in the ranks. When two engine drivers employed on the Manchester and Liverpool Railway came out on strike in support of a victimised colleague in 1836, they were charged with breach of contract and sentenced to a month's hard labour on the treadmill. A strike of two hundred and forty footplatemen in 1840 on the London and North Western was crushed by the use of blacklegs borrowed from other companies, as was a strike of a thousand members of the Engine Drivers and Firemen's United Society on the North Eastern in 1867. It was not until the formation of the

VAN GUARD   HEAD PORTER   CLOAK ROOM PORTER   T
      CARMAN   GENERAL PORTER   STATION SUPT'S CLE

Amalgamated Society of Railway Servants in 1872 and Associated Society of Locomotive Engineers and Firemen in 1880 that the trade unions made any substantial advances.

A large number of recruits were made among the railway workers because of the efforts of the union to reduce the terrible accident rate on the railways. Between 1875 and 1899, 12,870 men were killed at work and 68,575 injured. When asked by a Royal Commission what compensation there was for a widow whose husband was killed on the railways, a goods guard of the Taff Vale Railway replied 'I believe the compensation they receive is a nice coffin.' He was right. Arising from a strike for shorter hours by the ASRS (Scotland) in 1890, the nation was stirred by the accounts of excessive working and Parliament was moved towards control of railwaymen's hours. Accounts were cited of a signal box worker on the GWR who in a period of 310 days had worked 217 turns of 12 hours or more, 47 turns of 16 hours or more and one of over 20 hours. A goods guard, killed while shunting on a dark stormy night, had been on duty for twenty-two hours and eighteen minutes continuously, and a worker killed while fog signalling on the Brighton Line had been working for twenty-three hours in dense fog and bitterly cold weather. As a result of a prolonged and determined campaign by the ASRS accident figures declined from one in 334 in 1875 to one in 1,006 by 1889 though the toll was still horrendous.

Despite the harsh conditions of employment, the poor pay (as late as 1907, 100,000 had a standard weekly wage of under £1 per week) and the long hours, railwaymen were skilled and dedicated workers giving undue loyalty to their companies and engine drivers had immense personal pride in their own engines, brass and steel shining through the soot, smoke and steam.

The photographs are of one section of a three-part shot taken in 1881 of staff of the London Brighton and South Coast Railway and the staff of the North Eastern Railway at Fence Houses, County Durham, taken about 1880.

This nineteenth century group of workers posed at the quayside are coal trimmers and the most important tools of their trade were muscle and the curved shafted pointed shovels they proudly display.

Coal trimmers stored the coal into the holds and bunkers of ships, evenly and skilfully distributing the load so that the vessel would not list during the voyage. It was a filthy and obnoxious trade where working conditions were wretched and injurious to health. Coal would be shot on board down wooden chutes and thick clouds of dust would arise like an explosion as each new load landed, blinding and choking the men in the hold. They worked by candlelight and when standing close to the candles would be fortunate to see a mate two yards away. A coal trimmer who had been a miner once said that he swallowed more dust in a day in the ship than he had in twenty-four years down the pit. The trimmers could be recognised away from work by their curious coughs, a wheeze deep in the throat, a rattle of death.

The men formed a union at Cardiff in 1888 and by 1895, about the time this picture was taken, had thirteen hundred members. The union finally amalgamated with the Transport and General Workers' Union in 1968.

The explosion at the Roberts, Dale & Co. chemical works at Cornbrook, near Manchester on 22 June 1887, occurred during the Jubilee celebrations for Queen Victoria. Because of the royal event, only a dozen men were at work in the factory which was normally operated by more than seventy. Nevertheless, a worker was killed and the explosion was powerful enough to blast a baby from her cradle in a nearby cottage, the sound of the detonation being heard over an area of twenty miles.

The works were producing picric acid used for dyeing and picrate powder was commonly used in blasting because it was easy to detonate. Situated in a densely populated area, the company was guilty of breaking the sparse factory regulations of the age by illegally producing chemicals of an explosive nature. Although there were no warning notices about the danger of explosive chemicals in the factory and indeed the company denied at the subsequent inquest that they knew they were producing substances of an explosive nature, they succeeded in blaming the tragedy on a labourer for smoking a pipe. The accused and his mates strenuously denied the allegation but on 4 August 1887 the court put the blame on the employee for smoking, the company being mildly rebuked for not being aware of the chemical properties of what they were manufacturing. There was no compensation paid to the family of the man killed in the disaster.

The construction of the Thirlmere Aqueduct was started in 1878 to carry water from Mardale to Manchester to meet the increased demand for water for both domestic and industrial use. It was an ambitious scheme and included more than thirteen miles of tunnels and thirty-seven miles of cut and cover. The work of hacking through the countryside and boring through the hills was carried out by an army of navvies, many of whom were Irish immigrants. They lived on the job, some with their wives and children, for the work was to take sixteen years to complete. The conditions were appalling, the single men herded into barrack-like huts, the families in shanties and shacks that were freezing in the winter and stifling in the summer. Isolated in the country, away from the towns, without transport, the navvies were ready victims for the shanty town landlord and tommy shop owner. For most of the year the camp was set in a sea of mud and during the long cold winter evenings drinking was the only escape.

The work was hard and dangerous, it does not take a close study of the photograph to observe the primitive method of shoring the tunnel and accidents were an inevitable part of the job. Just how commonplace injury was may be judged by the following extract from a letter sent by a religious organisation, The Navvies Mission, to the men working on the Glaston Tunnel in the same year. 'Perhaps you will be killed suddenly by a fall of earth, by the blasting of a rock, by the crushing blow of an engine, by a bruise which may fester and mortify and poison the life blood. . . .' The answer, they claimed, was to turn to God.

A far larger engineering project than the Thirlmere Aqueduct was the construction of the 36½ mile long Manchester Ship Canal, linking England's second city to the Mersey estuary. Work started on 11 November 1887 and sixteen thousand men were employed on the scheme which took seven years to complete. Extensive use was made of earth-moving machinery and the photograph shows workers with one of the massive Ruston and Proctor steam navvies, *The Victory*, weighing almost one hundred tons. In one record-breaking day, such a machine filled six hundred and forty wagons in twelve hours, some two thousand five hundred tons being excavated.

The work was conducted at a furious pace, often continuing throughout the night by the light of Wells' pneumatic oil lights. In addition to the Ruston and Proctor steam navvies, Whittaker's excavators, Priestman grabs and German, French and American steam navvies were utilised in the shock assault upon the country-side. Ripping through clay, granite, spongy moss and sandy soil, the infantry of the attack were the navvies themselves, where men using the gin horse moved a hundred barrowfuls an hour, working to exhaustion for fourpence halfpenny an hour. In 1890, seven hundred of the men working on the section near Eccles, threatened to strike if they were not paid sixpence an hour, the Labourers' Union calling fourpence halfpenny 'boys wages'. The men also called for navvy representation on the juries sitting at inquests on the many fatal accidents arising from the work. The men won their pay increase but could not alter the composition of the middle class juries.

Early in 1891, two thousand struck work on the Barton section for parity with the concreters who had just gained a halfpenny an hour. Blacklegs were brought in but were quickly driven off by a hail of stones from the angry strikers. Mr Hall, an official of the Navvies Union, urged the men to go back to work until they were organised and could call out all the men from Eastham to Manchester, but at a mass meeting the navvies voted to continue to strike. The directors of the Manchester Ship Canal Company told the men that they could work or go away, just as they pleased, confident that with thousands of unemployed in the area they could soon break the strike. The men, totally without resources, did drift back to work but the unrest continued and the increase was eventually wrested from the company.

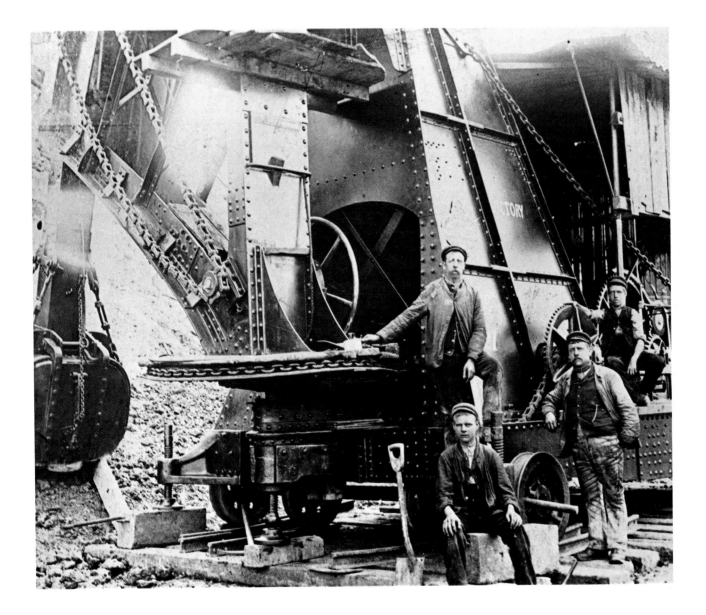

Thomas Burns was surface manager of Ackers Whiteley Colliery, Wigan, when this picture of him with his gang of 'pit brow lasses' was taken during the last decade of the nineteenth century. Burns, from Chadwicks' farm, Abram, close by to Wigan worked at the same pit for fifty-eight years and died on 26 August 1900 at the age of seventy-five. His pit brow lasses, known in Cumberland as 'screen lasses' and in South Wales as 'tip girls', worked at the colliery surface (underground work for women being made illegal in 1842) at a variety of jobs, screening coal, helping load and thrutch tubs and acting as pointswomen or greasers. Most of the girls were single or young widows, working for the same reason as the mill girls—necessity. The work was dirty and dangerous and there were a number of attempts by well meaning middle class reformers to ban women from such work. From north of Haydock to Wigan and just beyond, the girls wore clogs, trousers and short aprons, the trousers being considered by Victorian bourgeois society to be an affront to decency and conducive to immorality, the pit girls knew them to be warm and safer near moving machinery than voluminous skirts. The unions often attacked the use of female labour at the pits because of their exploitation as cheap labour. In 1886, when a man would earn two shillings and sixpence per day, the women were paid between one shilling and one shilling and sixpence and there were those who argued that the women worked twice as hard as the men.

A survey held in the same year showed that there were four thousand, one hundred and thirty-one women employed at the collieries, many working in conditions of appalling hardship and some even being employed on nightwork, despite the fact that nightwork for women had been illegal since 1872.

'North and South United' proclaimed a banner carried at the opening of the Woolwich Free Ferry on 23 March 1889. Bowler hatted trades unionists in their Sunday best led a half mile long procession of trade unions, friendly societies and trade societies while thousands thronged the decorated streets to welcome the free link across the Thames from Woolwich North to Woolwich South. Prior to the opening, the only means of crossing for many working people was by the Great Eastern Company's boat at a cost of a shilling a week plus tax for those who made the daily journey; hence the jubilation of the local populace.

At the opening ceremony, by Lord Rosebery, the link was hailed not only as a means of improved communication for work, but also as easier access to Epping Forest, which Queen Victoria had dedicated 'for the enjoyment of my people for all time' in 1878. 'The good time has come' said another banner reflecting the happy spirit of the occasion, though the opening was not without incident and was marred by the mounted police who charged over a pavement without warning into the densely packed crowd to the jeers and boos of the other onlookers.

The trade union banner in the photograph would seem to be that of a shipbuilders' union and was no doubt carried and followed by members who had worked on the building of the two boats which operated the ferry.

'There can be nothing ennobling in an atmosphere where we are huddled and herded together like cattle. There is nothing refining in the thought that to obtain employment we are driven into a shed, iron barred from end to end, outside of which a contractor or a foreman walks up and down with the air of a dealer in a cattle market, picking and choosing from a crowd of men who in their eagerness to obtain employment, trample each other underfoot, and where they fight like beasts for the chance of a day's work.' This description of dockers waiting for 'call on' was written by Ben Tillett in a little pamphlet entitled *A Dock Labourer's Bitter Cry* in July 1887. The casual work for which the starving dockers fought was paid at fourpence or fivepence an hour. It was Tillett's little union, the Tea Operatives and General Labourers' Association, formed by twelve men in the Oak Tavern off Hackney Road that was to lead the revolt that fired the Thames with the great strike for the 'dockers' tanner' in 1889.

On Monday, 12 August 1889, two members of the branch, meeting at Wroot's Coffee House, came to Tillett with a demand that they should declare a strike at the South West India Dock.

Though Tillett had campaigned for two years at the docks with an evangelical fervour, the demand surprised him. 'Was it possible to strike with men who shivered with hunger and cold, bullied and intimidated by the petty tyrants who took a delight in the brutalities of the call on?' The men left Tillett in no doubt as to the answer. Meetings were held under the windows of the dock offices and seethed with tumult. The demands included the raising of wages to sixpence an hour—'The full round orb of the dockers' tanner', as John Burns was to describe it, eightpence an hour for overtime and a reduction in the number of call ons, which kept hungry men hanging about the dock gates all day, often in the wet and cold awaiting the next chance to catch the foreman's eye. The strike spread rapidly throughout the docks, stevedores, boilermakers, coal heavers, ballastmen, lightermen, painters and carpenters all supporting the dock labourers. With only seven shillings and sixpence in his union funds, Tillett set about raising money to provide relief for the striking dockers and their families. Daily marches with banners and bands around the docks and to the City served to keep up morale, spread the news and keep money pouring into the jingling collecting boxes. Donations came

from all sections of the community, employees of the Savoy Hotel sent one pound eighteen shillings and sixpence, two Paddington firewood cutters sent one pound, a shareholder in one of the dock companies, ten pounds, two poor bricklayers, two shillings. From the strike committee headquarters at the Wade's Arms, Ben Tillett, Tom Mann, Eleanor Marx, John Burns, Harry Orbell, Henry Champion and others planned the distribution of the money.

Champion persuaded the strike committee to issue one shilling food tickets and local tradesmen to honour them. Tom Mann took charge of the task and tells in his memoirs how he faced the first crowd of anxious hungry dockers, 'I put my back against one of the doorposts and stretched out my leg, with my foot on the opposite post, jamming myself in. I talked pleasantly to the men and passed each man in under my leg!' 'I can see Tom now, with his back against the door of Wroot's Coffee House', wrote Tillett, 'keeping back a yelling, hungry mob, while Nash and Smith shivered in the pay room.' Eight relief centres were established, tickets being issued on production of a union card. This was not only a rational way of issuing relief but served to build the union, twenty thousand cards being issued for the twopenny entrance fee in this way.

Contemporary reports tell of women and children feeding in the streets and the photograph taken during the strike shows women with their meal tickets pinned to their hats and dresses, feeding their children outside one of the union centres. At the peak of the struggle, twenty-five thousand meal tickets a day were being issued by the union.

Eventually on 14 September 1889 a settlement favourable to the dockers was reached. The Tea Operatives Union which began the strike with a few hundred members, finished it with a membership of eighteen thousand and the ground was prepared for the building of the great Dockers' Union, the Dock, Wharf, Riverside and General Labourers' Union of Great Britain and Ireland.

The photograph shows victorious strikers, greeting the end of the strike, one of the most significant in the history of British trades unionism.

1890

'God bless the squire and all his relations and keep us in our proper stations' was the end of many a prayer in rural churches where life was ordained by the unholy trinity of Squire, Parson and Farmer. Joseph Arch, founder of the first national trade union for farmworkers, the National Agricultural Labourers' Union in 1872, described his first glimpse of a communion service, 'First up walked the squire to the communion rails, the farmers went up next, then up went the tradesmen, the shopkeepers, the wheelwright, the blacksmith and then, very last of all the agricultural labourers.'

It was against this triple tyranny that the farm labourers struggled to build trade unionism in the countryside. Added to that tyranny was the circumstance of isolation, both at work and in the nature of village life. A man might work alone in the fields from dawn till dusk, a life of unremitting toil unrelieved by holidays for a wage of £12 a year if a labourer or £20 if 'a good head waggoner'. Even when working alongside his fellows he saw little of the world beyond his master's farm, the primitive tied cottage in which he lived and a semblance of social life at the village pub. Nor did he share in the fruits of the earth on which he toiled; the harvester who killed a rabbit bolting from the last of the corn could find himself before the local magistrate, invariably a farmer.

It took a special kind of courage to stand with a few labouring brothers and sing

> Ye tillers of the soil
> Assert your manhood then,
> You get your living by hard toil,
> Then all be union men.

The workers of Laird Bros. built the *Royal Oak* at Birkenhead and the photograph of the assembled Lairds, their ladies and their workers was recorded for posterity by Mr Petree, a draughtsman who worked for the firm. The gathering was assembled at the keel-laying ceremony on 29 May 1890, indeed, the work had to be hurried so that the keel would be declared laid on 'Royal Oak Day'. The sign seen in the photograph gives the ship's dimensions, length 375 feet, breadth 75 feet, depth 49 feet 10 inches, displacement 14,300 tons, and is bordered with oak leaves. Below the board can be seen a small branch of oak given by Mrs Gladstone to David Charles Davies, one of Lairds' oldest employees.

At noon, Mr and Mrs William Laird, accompanied by John Laird and Miss Laird, together with the Admiralty overseer, Mr Millard and a number of the principal foremen inspected the work and William Laird declared the 200 foot keel duly laid. This was a keel of exceptional size and the number five dock at Lairds had to be specially lengthened to accommodate the huge vessel.

The directors pose, confident in their knowledge that Britain will continue to rule the waves. The shipworkers? Well, the thumbs in the waistcoat give an indication of pride, though most of the others seem to show the expected degree of humility. Contrast the central figure of the worker wearing the bowler with the haughty expression of the lady in the top row, second from the right. Each in their place?

The poses of their skills held by the Sussex coopers for the time exposure belies the physical strength and manual dexterity required for the craft. The intense heat of a cooper's shop, caused by the fire from the cresset, lit to make the staves pliable enough for bending, the muscle required to work bone-hard Persian oak, one end on the block hook, the other pushed firmly into the stomach as three foot shavings are peeled by the hollowing knife and the booming crash of a flogger driving a chime hoop onto a cask cannot be captured by the camera.

In the nineteenth century, barrels were used for the packing of commodities of every kind, herrings, chinaware, nails, sugar and gunpowder, dry goods as well as wet. A country cooper would make wooden pails as the last verse of an old cooper's shop sign testifies

> I make and mend both tub and cask,
> And hoop 'em strong to make them last,
> Here's butter prints and butter scales
> And butter boards and milking pails.

Coopers' trade unions in the nineteenth century consisted of small societies, each specialising in a different branch of the trade. The 'Hand-in-Hand', for example, formed in 1824, organised molasses coopers, mainly in the West India Docks.

'White Coopers' covered those on 'Whitework', the making of wooden buckets, tubs, harness casks and fancy work. Virtually every town in which casks were made had its own society, The Glasgow Coopers' Friendly Society, Liverpool Coopers' Operative Society, Bristol Friends of Humanity, for example, and in some cities the trade was large enough to support two or more societies who were fiercely sectarian and deadly rivals. An attempt was made in 1854 to bring unity by the formation of a National Association of Coopers and although it lasted for fourteen years it never conquered the local societies jealous regard for their own autonomy. A London society in the 1860s affiliated to the First International and various 'Amalgamated' and 'National' unions followed over the years, but invariably carried the old feuds and town jealousies with them.

The great lock-out of 1893 lasted from July to September and was marked by the dreadful deprivation suffered by the miners and their families and by the widespread use of troops and imported police forces against the colliers. The mineowners sought to impose a twenty-five percent reduction in wages and the men, by ballot, overwhelmingly voted against acceptance of such a drastic cut in their already meagre pay. The owners responded by closing the pits, looking to starvation to force their terms on the Miners' Federation. More than a quarter of a million men were locked out or struck in solidarity.

The unions did not have the funds to provide for the sustenance of their members and hasty arrangements were made to lessen the distress inflicted on the women and children. Soup kitchens were set up in all districts and appeals made for public support. Sympathy was widespread and many surprising acts of individual assistance are recorded. At Bulwell, Nottinghamshire, two local churches paid the proceeds of their Sunday collections to the union fund while the editor of *The Nottingham Daily Express* backed the call for help and gifts poured into his newspaper office. Despite the help given by local tradesmen, public donations and collections of food, hunger began to bite as the weeks without money became months of black misery. With hunger came desperate and often violent opposition to the introduction of blackleg labour into some of the smaller pits. Blacklegs were stoned, colliery rail trucks overturned and burned out, in one instance a blackleg was paraded through the streets of Radford with a symbolic rope around his neck. The response of the wealthy and often titled owners was a demand for troops and police to be drafted for the protection of their property and the coercion of the miners. A special train left London for Alfreton carrying the Second Dragoon Guards, to support the eight hundred red-jacketed Royal Irish Fusiliers already there, while in

Wentworth Woodhouse
Great Coal Strike 1893

Chippenham the police appeared wearing cutlasses! Throughout the coalfields, troops in unprecedented numbers and police forces from far-away counties arrived without delay. The influx of the well-dressed, well-fed soldiers aroused great indignation in the poor mining villages. At Chesterfield, pinched faced hungry children watched at the soldiers' tented camp while the cook dropped large lumps of fresh meat and vegetables into the cookpot. By the roadside outside, stood 'two hungry white faced men, guarding a basket with a board bearing the inscription "Chesterfield Trades and Labour Council collection in aid of miners." ' It was against a background of hunger and repression that a terrible tragedy was contrived at Featherstone at Aktons Hall Colliery owned by Lord Masham. The men had an agreement with the manager that trucks of 'smudge' would not be moved. When the agreement was broken, feeling ran high and several trucks were overturned. Lord St. Oswald, the owner of a neighbouring colliery

and also a JP, sent to York for the military. By the same afternoon, Captain Barker and twenty-eight infantrymen were at the colliery, the starving miners further incensed by the sight of the uniformed soldiers parading the cobbled streets. At 6 p.m. a great crowd gathered at the colliery and demanded that the troops should depart and they did in fact leave for the railway station, only to be sent back again by a magistrate. The crowd grew larger and stones were thrown, the Riot Act read and still the crowd stood firm. The magistrate ordered the troops to fire and two men were killed and sixteen wounded, British workers shot down by British soldiers. The photographs show cavalry quartered at the stately home of Wentworth Woodhouse, the seat of the Earl of Stafford, William Fitzwilliam, an honorary Colonel of the 1st West Yorkshire Yeoman Cavalry and police imported to Pleasley Colliery on the Nottinghamshire-Derbyshire border from Montgomery in Wales.

DEFENCE NOT DEFIANCE.
Pleasley Colliery, October, 1893.

It was almost certainly a Sunday morning when members of the Mersey Quay and Railway Carters' Union assembled complete with horses and cart outside the studios of the photographer Hinchcliffe in Cazneau Street, Liverpool, in 1897. The head office of the union was just down the road at number thirty-five and one is left to speculate as to whether the carters, dressed in Sunday best, are about to set off on a beano or have arranged to commemorate the unfurling of their new banner.

There were some five thousand men employed in carting goods from quayside to railway sidings or warehouses when the union was founded on 1 March 1890. Conditions of work were grim, with excessive hours, heavy labour, low pay and the whip of unemployment held over those who complained. When William Almond, the founder of the union, called his first meeting under the lamp at Lambeth Road, Kirkdale, only nine men came for fear of the masters. In a typical day's work, a carter would rise at four thirty in the morning and reach the stables soon after five. His first task was to feed the horses and bed up the straw before he brewed himself a can of tea and had a quick slice of bread for breakfast. Then, it was clean the harness and horses, harness up and away, for the object was to be 'first on turn' at the quay. It was first come, first served, and to be at the end of the queue could mean a wait of two or three hours. Contacting the 'counter-off', the boss of the cargo and establishing his turn was vital to an early start. The cart would be loaded and the first of the day's journeys made from ship to railway or warehouse, offload, back again until the quota was completed at seven in the evening. The only break was dinner, seldom an hour as the first duty of the carter was to water and nosebag his horses. He never left his horses, for an unattended horse could mean prosecution and a fine of ten shillings. His last work of the day would be to put in an hour's work at the stable for no pay. An average day's work was fifteen hours, the pay, twenty-six shillings if working with a single horse or twenty-nine shillings for a team. That was the union rate, for those outside, the pay was invariably lower.

The great South Wales strike of miners was two months old when this picture was taken in June 1898 of strikers from Ty Trist and Whitworth collieries. The dispute arose over the demand of the men to end the system of sliding scale payments which aided cut-throat competition and had 'no bottom' to the scale. The miners claimed a ten percent advance and a guaranteed minimum selling price of coal at ten shillings a ton.

The owners were particularly obdurate in their refusal to negotiate and when the Home Secretary appointed Sir Edward Fry as official conciliator, the coal owners bluntly told Sir Edward that they could not tolerate his intervention and he swallowed the rebuff and returned to London.

The miners had little funds but massive support was given by the trade unions. Colliers working at non-associated pits won an increase of ten percent and their entire increase was sent to the strikers. The relief fund paid out more that £5,000 a week to the strikers and their families but despite this there was much hardship and instances are recorded of miners being fined by the magistrates for poaching and stealing food. Troops were drafted to the area, thirty-four officers and seven hundred and sixty-two men being sent at the request of the Chief Constable of Monmouthshire. The Home Secretary was asked in the House if he was aware that the stipendary magistrate for the Pontypridd Petty Sessional Division had received a letter from the local Justices of the Peace commanding him to instruct the military detachments, if necessary, to charge the crowd, to use the bayonet and to fire with ball cartridges? Despite minor incidents there was no real unrest and the strike lasted until 1 September 1898, when the men returned after five months of privation, largely on the owners' terms.

It is believed that the miners in the photograph found work during the strike breaking quarry rock for local road building, hence the array of hammers.

In the 1840s, John Pounds, a crippled cobbler of Portsmouth, used to gather in his workshop little groups of the poorest boys he could find, teaching them to read while he continued with his repairs. Pounds' educational work and that of the London City Mission, who started schools into which 'children raggedly clothed are admitted', were the originators of the evangelical mission which became known as the Ragged Schools' Union. The mission was to rescue children who were the 'street arabs' and outcasts of the poorest working class districts and provide them with education and recreation. It was into the London of Dickens' Oliver Twist that they delved to find and rescue children from the worst effects of indescribable poverty and abandonment. Indeed, Dickens was to support and write of the work of the Ragged Schools, a movement that was to attract other reforming figures like Shaftesbury, Quentin Hogg and Barnado.

Finding that their pupils were often 'crying from hunger and falling from their seats through exhaustion', the Ragged Schools gave meals as often as possible. About the time that the photograph of 'ragged children' with their teacher was taken, the Camberwell Ragged School announced 'bring a spoon'. Two hundred and fifty children sat at rows of long tables and were given a slice of bread and a basin of soup thickened with peas and barley, at the cost of a halfpenny. Though the purpose of the Ragged Schools was education for Church and Empire, they also filled empty bellies and cared for those for whom society had no care.

James Wild (centre, with beard) was born in 1844 and worked as a mule spinner at the Millbrook Spinning Mill near Oldham when this photograph was taken during the 1890s. Mule spinners regarded themselves as aristocrats of labour and were strongly organised into militant all male trade unions in contrast to other sections of the textile industry where there was a preponderance of organised women workers. Cotton spinners were among the earliest workers to form trade unions and were initially organised into local societies based on mill towns. There is reference to the Friendly Society of Cotton Spinners of Stockport in 1785 and the various societies came together to hold the first 'Spinners' Parliament' in 1829.

Entry to the trade was jealously controlled and the spinners were often responsible for hiring, firing and paying their assistants, 'big piecers' and 'little piecers', acting as a type of sub-contractor to the mill owner. Boys like those seen in the photograph would start work as little piecers, sweeping and cleaning and look to progressing eventually to become fully fledged minders. In 1893, boys could be employed as half timers at eleven years of age for five hours a day and would rise at five in the morning to trudge on dark winter mornings to work barefoot in the humid atmosphere of the mill before attending school in a state of exhaustion in the afternoons. It was not until the Education Act of 1918 that the half time system was finally abolished.

Industrial diseases were common among cotton workers and James Wild finally became a victim of cotton cancer, caused by skin penetration of the oil used to lubricate the mules and died in 1902. The disease was finally recognised as a prescribed industrial disease through the efforts of the Amalgamated Association of Operative Cotton Spinners and Twiners in 1946.

In addition to the meals provided by the Ragged Schools, the 'slum sisters' of the Salvation Army offered farthing breakfasts to poor children, particularly in East London. The purpose was to provide a basic meal at the start of the day for children who would otherwise have gone to school with empty stomachs. A huge mug of hot sweet tea and a doorstep of bread and jam would be given in exchange for the smallest coin of the realm to children to whom the best meal of the day might well have been stale bread covered with putrid dripping or a red herring with pickles. Skimmed milk and a pennyworth of brawn or cold potatoes and potted meat would commonly serve as the main meal for the children of East London and the even less fortunate would have to scour the market places for rotten vegetables and fruit discarded as unsaleable.

The practice of supplying farthing meals was continued by the Salvation Army in the depressed areas until the 1930s. Farthing teas were provided in the Rhondda where the children would bring a penny on Monday and be given bread, jam, cocoa and three tickets to last until Thursday. Friday was 'dole day' and a meal would be assured at home.

JOHN PEARSON.

The Crippled Shoemaker from Ringstead, who marched at the head of the procession of the "RAUNDS STRIKERS" from Raunds to London and back.
MAY, 1905.   COLES. *Photographer, Watford*

1900

The relief of Mafeking on 17 May 1900, was followed in Britain with such scenes of patriotic jubilation as to give a new word to the English language. In the Royal Small Arms Factory, Enfield, the workers organised in the Amalgamated Society of Engineers needed no prompting to hurl themselves into a fit of khaki madness in the celebration of the imperial victory.

As the rumour of the lifting of the siege began to filter through men hammered on their benches. In the machine-gun shop, the foreman on hearing the news ordered the engine to be stopped, called the men together and announced the momentous tidings. 'They gave three cheers and sang God Save the Queen.' 'We ought to do something' came the cry from the men that made the guns that beat the Boers. A party of a hundred with brooms and shovels paraded as a mock army through the smiths' shop and into the large workshop. The foreman unacquainted with the situation stared in amazement, eyes glistening as men picked up lances, produced flags, found swords and banged sheets of iron to arouse the entire factory. Smiths in their aprons, machine men in white aprons and engineers in blue and white jackets joined the march to 'Soldiers of the Queen', cheers, cheers, cheers and the National Anthem. 'What would old Kruger say if he saw this?' The revelries were carried outside to the house of the manager where they sang 'Land of Hope and Glory' and then on into the night to church bells, bonfires, fireworks and bugle blowing pande-monium. A local paper described 'paroxysms of unrestrained delight' and printed an apt piece of doggerel

> Theirs is not to reason why
> Theirs is but to cheer and cry
> Hurrah for Baden Powell!

They might better have quoted the cynical imperialist comment of Sir Alfred Milner—'You have only to sacrifice the nigger and the game is easy.'

Dressed like dukes, treated like slaves. Shop assistants, earning as little as thirty pounds a year, were expected to dress like aristocrats and spend their lives in total subjection to their employers. Almost half a million were compelled to 'live in' their employers' premises in conditions which were appalling and institutional. Behind the palatial facades of the great stores staffed by seemingly obsequious dummies the shopowners created a tyranny as harsh as the yearly bond system of the mineowners or the feudal power of the squirarchy. Stores were open from morning to night for six days a week and working hours of eighty to ninety hours a week were common. The campaign of the Shop Assistants' Union for a *sixty hour week* did not begin until 1909.

The 'living in' system bound the shopworker to the shopowner as tightly as the tied cottage bound the labourer to the farm owner. Much of the accommodation was barrack-like with beds alive with fleas and walls crawling with bugs. Stories proliferate of the unfortunate occupants pouring paraffin on mattresses and filling cracks in the walls with soap. Baths were rarely provided and hot water was almost as scarce. Communal sitting rooms were as spartan as railway waiting-rooms and the lives of the impecunious assistants were governed by petty regulations enforced by fines. The rules of one Knightsbridge store forbade pictures or photographs in the bedrooms. Anyone having a light on after 11 p.m. was instantly dismissed. Sleeping out without permission was forbidden, the first offence incurring a fine of two shillings and sixpence, the second, dismissal.

At William Whiteley's store in London, absentees from work had to put their name and department on a notice board together with their reason for absence. Whiteley himself would then add his comment; thus, Smith, Silks, unwell, 'no he is not, he is a lazy fellow!' Assistants were forbidden to marry without permission and communal living deprived them of the vote. On their one free day they were expected to go to church.

The photograph, taken in May 1901, shows thirteen shop assistants from William Whiteley's advertising a meeting against the 'living in' system with sandwich boards hired from the Church Army. Leading the procession is Duncan Davies from the drapery department. Third in line is P.C. Hoffman, a pioneer of the Shop Assistants' Union, and a trade union official for forty years.

This print, taken from a Social Democratic Federation lantern slide shows an aspect of outcast London that alarmed the middle class. Each night winter and summer alike, thousands slept in the open in the public places of the metropolis, an outward manifestation of the unemployment, poverty and shocking housing that existed in the capital city of the Empire.

Charitable institutions were unable to cope with the vast numbers that sought nightly entrance to their refuges and many of the outcast lacked even the few coppers required for common lodging houses and 'dossers'. Others preferred the open streets to the casual ward where they ran the risk of being detained for three days against their will and there were hundreds who would chance the exposure to the elements rather than submit to the workhouse. In the 1880s, Trafalgar Square was a popular venue, the Vestry of St. Martin's-in-the-Fields complaining to the Commissioner of Police of 'unseemly conduct of persons sleeping at night in Trafalgar Square and performing their ablutions in the morning in the basins and fountains.' It was by no means unusual for three or four hundred people to sleep in the Square on a fine night. Following the SDF organised demonstrations of the poor and unemployed in Trafalgar Square in 1887, the authorities finally banned the Square to the homeless. The embankment, with its seats and bridges, continued to be used, mothers with babies in arms, children and old people regularly to be seen spending the night insulated against the cold with old newspapers and sacks. The thousands who slept out were not for the most part derelicts of drink, but honest, poor, unskilled and casual workers, subject to seasonal and trade fluctuations of employment. General Booth in *Darkest London* quotes a typical case of a Bethnal Green bootmaker, in hospital for three months. His wife also became ill and after three weeks their furniture was seized for the rent due to the landlord. Subsequently, they were evicted. Too ill to work, everything pawned, including the precious tools of his trade, they became the dispossessed, outcasts of society.

Not coffins—beds! This photograph could have been taken in any one of a number of night refuges at the turn of the century. Most likely it was taken at Medland Hall, a London Congregational Union refuge in the heart of East London's dockland. The shelter contained three hundred and forty-three coffin-like beds, yet such were the numbers of destitutes in the metropolis that as many as six or seven hundred hapless souls would begin queuing hours before the doors opened at seven in the evening. The beds held mattresses made of dry seaweed encased in leathercloth and were laid out in neat rows, each bed numbered, in perfect order. Every man would be provided with a lump of bread and butter on arrival and prodigious quantities of boiling water were available for the making of tea, many men bringing with them old tea leaves which had been used and used again. Admission was by a small charge, usually, twopence, and evening and morning prayers were compulsory. Other refuges were free, 'No man need beg, starve, steal or commit suicide' read a placard outside a Salvation Army shelter at Blackfriars.

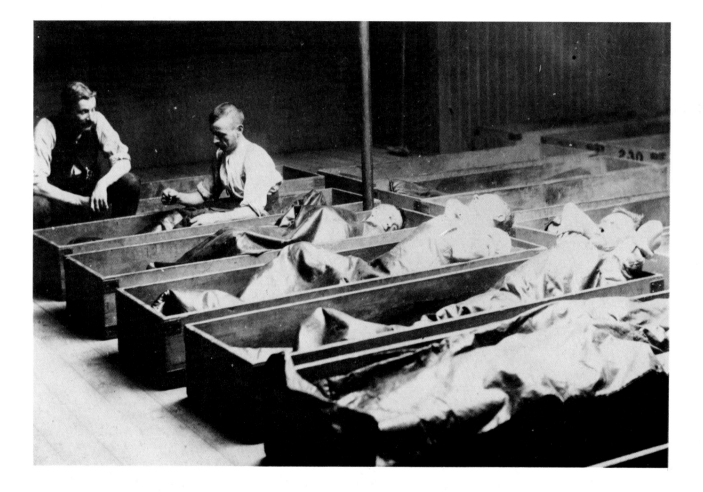

If the leathercloth beds were comfortable, the material being hard, cold and non-porous, it seems that American cloth used in some institutions was even worse. Getting into a bunk was likened to 'climbing between two icicles' and the following morning the 'dosser' would find the material sticking to his skin due to its non-porosity. It had the merit of being easily washed and disinfected and the experienced soon learned to put a barrier of newspaper between themselves and the provided covering.

Other shelters were run by the Church of England and the Church Army. The night refuge at Providence Row, East London, founded by the Revd Dr Gilbert, received nightly three hundred men, and children, and for cleanliness a huge bath, three yards long, was provided and used by a dozen inmates simultaneously. The food here was said to be superior, bread and cocoa being provided night and morning.

Not all the 'dossers' were out of work, many were simply homeless and earned such poor wages that renting rooms was beyond their means. Records from Medland Hall showed sailors, firemen, painters, bricklayers and shoemakers among those who sought shelter from the inhospitable streets of the richest city in the world.

The next four photographs are of London children, two taken for the Salvation Army, one for the Social Democratic Federation and the other from an album in the Fawcett Library and used by George Sims in his volumes on *Living London.* They must all be seen as pictures purposely taken to demonstrate aspects of poverty, though that does not detract from the help they give us in appreciating the effects and extent of poverty in the capital city in an age of imperial splendour.

Elementary education had been compulsory since 1880, but most poor children worked. The report of the Inter-Departmental Committee on the Employment of Schoolchildren, in 1901, put the figure at three hundred thousand children in England and Wales combining school attendance with paid employment. If that is a fact, it does not convey the devastating effect on the health and education of working class children inadequately or badly fed, invariably badly dressed, totting up a sixteen hour day of school-work and labour. Reports of children falling from their desks with exhaustion or fainting from hunger were common and it does not require more than a modicum of imagination to picture the condition of bare footed, raggedly clothed children arriving at school in wet or wintry weather, having already put in a few hours work, often in the open air. Look closely at the photograph from the Fawcett album of schoolchildren in a playground and those with boots are seen to be scarcely better shod than those who are barefooted. School authorities were not unaware of the problem and as early as 1879 the London School Board began to provide boots for the poorest children in order that they could attend school, only to find themselves attacked by the Charity Organisation Society who feared that other parents would keep their children at home in order to obtain boots. The problem of the poor in providing boots for their children was to remain a source of concern until the outbreak of the Second World War, while the philosophy expounded by the COS has persisted to limit help for the underprivileged in the Welfare State.

Work for children was a necessity born of unemployment, casual labour, trade recessions, seasonal occupations, and the payment of less than subsistence wages, not only in the sweated trades but by the employers in the major sections of British commerce, including dockwork, mining and agriculture. What of the work that the children undertook in their playtime? Helping the milkman from four thirty in the morning till schooltime and again from five till nine, selling newspapers for sixty hours a week, lather boy to the barber from school-out till ten every night, delivering heavy groceries, paid at 'thruppence for six hours', these extra chores contributed to the family income and in some cases, where dad was out of work and the family large, was the family income, saving them from the final degradation of the workhouse. The photograph taken by the SDF of the little girl collecting or delivering a fourpenny bag of coke may be just an errand or an incident during a gas works strike, it is uncertain. It could well be work, for girls of that age frequently worked before

and after school hours, just as their brothers. 'Door step' girls, some of them 'too small to reach the bell' would wash and whiten the front steps, blacklead the range or beat the mats for the better-off local shopkeepers and traders, taking payment not in money but in scraps of food. In the rural areas, little girls performing menial tasks for scraps of bread were known as 'hardcrust nannies'. A report from Glasgow tells of a ten year old girl working at a dairy from six till nine in the morning and from four thirty to seven in the evening, her bare feet like two pieces of frozen meat, all this for one and ninepence a week and still unable to buy herself shoes and stockings. A girl of thirteen with frail arms worked after school each day in a tinplate factory, carrying loads of thirty pounds in weight, while a boy of eleven worked in an undertaker's, his duties included measuring the corpses. Another boy helped the coalman, and came to school each day covered in coal dust.

Thousands of children spent their after-school hours around the

kitchen table helping with the manufacture of goods in the most sweated of all industries, 'outwork'. Here, beyond the organisation of trade unions, outside factory regulations, there was no limit to the hours to be worked, no minimum wage to be enforced, no restrictions concerning health and safety. Most of the work involved repetitive tasks of a simple kind and children worked as child slaves while their mothers worked for a pittance. The carding of hooks and eyes was an example of how children were involved in 'helping mother', providing the cheapest of cheap labour. While mum and the girls sewed the eyes on the cards, the boys and the babies would pass on the hooks, four dozen to a card and gross upon gross to be completed. A woman and a little girl told of starting on Saturday morning and after two days of tired eyes and sore fingers had earned one shilling and sixpence, the woman having to provide her own needles and the cotton! The drudgery was eternal.

The two photographs from the Salvation Army pose questions that suggest they were both contrived. The children outside the pie and eel shop seem poor (even if the boy in knickerbockers is better attired than his mates) but they have been able to make a purchase from the pie shop; perhaps the photographer rewarded his subjects. Nevertheless, the small sartorial details tell a story of handed down clothes and lack of footwear that was a common sight in the cities at that time. The mother and four children are posed with soup kitchen handouts, the enamel bowls, giant mug and 'doorsteps' providing the props for a picture of slumland life. Here the children appear well fed, even allowing for the probability that they dressed up for the occasion.

Taken together, the four pictures of children from three differing sources have a good deal in common and leave the viewer to reflect on childhood in working class London at the start of the present century.

In November 1886, the Revd Samuel Francis Collier was placed in charge of the new Methodist Central Hall, Manchester, built at the then prodigious cost of £40,000. Magnificent though the Hall was, the dynamic evangelist, with a social as well as a spiritual conscience, soon launched a programme of practical help for the poor, using the motto 'Need not creed' in his daring new ministry. Nobody in need was to be refused help, regardless of belief. In 1891, an old rag factory was established in Ancoats, salvaging the waste of the city, old bottles, jars, empty tins, cotton waste, pails and clothing all being sorted for re-use and sale, destitute and derelict men being given a good bed and three square meals a day for their labour. From that venture in social rehabilitation grew the most complete set of social service premises possessed by any church in Britain. By the early 1900s a Men's Home, Labour Yard, Women's Refuge, a Maternity Hospital for unmarried mothers and a Labour Advice Bureau had all been developed together with educational clubs, prison visiting services and holiday funds.

The picture of the boys shows them working at chopping firewood in the Labour Yard of the Manchester and Salford Wesleyan Missions. Outcasts of industrial society, they were welcomed by Collier and provided with clothes, food, shelter and hope in exchange for 'honest toil'.

'We all had to muck in and help with the housework. Oh that Lancashire cleanliness! That cleaning of the front step and flags. That scrubbing down of the backyard.' These were the words used by Harry Pollitt in describing his early life in the textile village of Droylsden, Lancashire. The photograph, taken in Scunthorpe, well illustrates the task of 'scrubbing the flags', it also illustrates the constant struggle of working class families living in industrial areas throughout Britain to combat the grime and continuous muck of the commercial surroundings in which they lived. Whitening the doorstep, washing the step and brushing or washing to the kerb was as common in the East End of London as it was in the Midlands and North.

Contrary to the Tory myth of 'coals in the bath' most working people fought continuously against the unbridled filth and pollution of free enterprise capitalism. Blackleading the stove, whitening the hearth, scrubbing the kitchen table, polishing the brass and washing and ironing was the daily lot of the majority of women, not only for their masters and mistresses, if they were 'in service', but for themselves and their children in everyday working life. The 'mangle' was aptly named, as in outhouse, scullery and backyard, they slaved to bring cleanliness and respectability to a life of deadening toil for their men and domestic drudgery for themselves. Their efforts were not only a doorstep facade but penetrated to the heart of the home as pinched and hungry women strove to patch, darn and mend garments seemingly beyond repair while their menfolk mended boots and freely repaired the landlords' houses.

Not every nineteenth century employer of labour was a natural-born despot. Companies such as Colman's of mustard fortune operated a benevolent form of capitalism, introducing education and insurance schemes years ahead of state compulsion.

In 1857 (thirteen years before the first real education act) when countless children toiled ten or twelve hours a day in mill or colliery, Jeremiah James Colman opened Carrow School for the children of his employees at Stoke and Carrow. The weekly payments were one penny for one child, three halfpence for two and twopence for three from the same family. The first school at Carrow was over a carpenter's shop, 'up an opening by the Red Lion Inn' and crammed in fifty-three pupils. In an opening statement, Colman said 'the school helps you to educate your children and to train up a set of men who will go into the world qualified for any duties they may be called upon to discharge.' With a workforce of three thousand five hundred, Colman's was in effect the local community and the likelihood was that their duties would be discharged in the manufacture of mustard. It was a family business not only in the usual sense of the expression, meaning owned by a family, but was staffed by many families. In fact it was said that the only way to get a job at Colman's was to be 'spoken for' by a relative already working there. With Victorian paternalism, Jeremiah James Colman, greatnephew of the founder, philanthropist and Member of Parliament ruled his 'family' with firm discipline but due regard for their welfare.

School began each morning with a hymn, a prayer and a Bible reading and although a Colman education included 'diligent and careful teaching of the scriptures' it also included art and craft subjects beyond the three r's. Far sighted in his attitude to education Colman was a staunch believer in women being given

every opportunity for learning, and from the outset drawing and needlework were included in the subjects taught.

Precluded by his business and parliamentary interests from taking as active a part as he may have wished in running the school, his wife Caroline became the force in the direction and development of the school. The Colmans were committed to technical education and by 1899 claimed to be the first in Norwich to introduce cookery, gardening, laundrywork, beekeeping and ironwork into the curriculum. As the years went by the school moved, expanded and improved, adding a wide range of technical subjects but never neglecting art and culture.

At the time the photographs were taken in the early 1900s Caroline Colman was intensely concerned with the physical well-being of her pupils, urging mothers to ensure that their daughters wore warm dresses with high tops and long sleeves 'as a caution against measles and other childish ailments'. Although the children have been carefully groomed and prepared for the class photograph, their general condition of well-being contrasts sharply with the ragged appearance and thin faces of the children in so many of the other scenes of this period.

The reminiscences of former pupils seem to be warm and dutifully grateful, happy and nostalgic, if at times a little pious. On a Whitsun fete day, 'the ham sandwiches and sponge cakes were "par excellence". When all was ready for tea we all stood up and the Carrow band played "Grace".'

One girl remembered 'my class was the cottage and I always sat on the back seat as I could turn round and sometimes watch my father coming down the hill to work. He was always a little late, it being one of his sins.'

Chainmaking and the Black Country are inseparably linked. By the beginning of this century, a thousand tons of chain a week, from the largest anchor chain to dog collars was being produced in Stourbridge, Dudley, Cradley Heath, Halesowen and Bromsgrove. The heavy chain, of the kind shown being unloaded from a railway wagon at the quayside, was made by men organised in the Amalgamated Society of Anchorsmiths and Shackle Workers, founded by pioneer labour leader Tom Stitch. Working in intense heat, sustained from dehydration by draughts of beer, the health of the chainmakers suffered severely from the fierce alternation of temperatures and the heavy nature of the industry. Robert Sherhard was told by a chainmaker from Cradley Heath 'the work affects you all over . . . you gets so cold that you shivers so that you can't hold your food. The furnaces burn your insides right out of you.' The man had burns all over his body, 'it's easier to catch a flea than a piece of red hot iron, and the bits of red hot iron are always flying about. Sometimes a bit gets into your boot and puts you "on the box" for a week.'

Wages at the turn of the century reached to a maximum of fifteen shillings a week for a working day of six hours, six days a week. The lighter chain was made by women and children working in small workshops with five or six women at the anvils or in family groups in sheds in their own backyards. The women chainmakers of Cradley Heath worked with seared and calloused hands while their children crawled around the floor amid the flying sparks. For twelve hours a day a woman would be paid from five shillings to eight shillings a week, working for a parasitic fogger, a middleman, or more often a middlewoman who wielded the power of low wages with the alternative choice of starvation.

The sympathy of the nation was aroused for the women chainmakers when Mary MacArthur of the National Federation of Women Workers led five hundred of them in a strike in 1910. The same year, a group of the women aroused the Trades Union Congress when they appeared on the platform, silently holding their chains, while one of them made a brief appeal for help.

Lesser known was the work in the Staffordshire brickfields of the 'clay dabber chicks', women who performed the same work as men with the deadweight, unyielding, glutinous clay. Working barefooted in small groups, they wheeled clay to the pug mills, moulded up to a thousand bricks a day, sweated in the stifling heat of the kiln shops and loaded barges for a wage of between six and ten shillings a week. The photograph of women brickmakers was taken at Stourbridge.

My name is Henry Gittus, that's my name on the machine. I own the firm and I live at Brook House, Chapel-en-le-Frith. That means I am worth some brass.

The photograph was taken in the Gittus shop at the Midland Iron Works, Travis Street, Manchester, and was probably taken as a publicity shot for the metal shearing machine featured in the tableau. Gittus made punching and shearing machinery at Travis Street between 1880 and 1930 and it is surely Henry Gittus that poses confidently on the left of the picture; just look at the assertive pride. Next, the smart pipe smoking young director, who, if not the boss's son, seems to exude 'the future is mine'. Alongside, another director or manager and dutifully posed at the foot of the machine, the operative.

Intended to demonstrate the solid reliability of machine and management, the picture unintentionally captures the class division between the employers and the employed.

Labour was cheap when this group of men were photographed excavating for the tramway in Tendarves Street, Tuckingmill, Camborne, Cornwall, in 1902. With pick, shovel and barrow, it was the muscle and sinew of men that linked Camborne with Redruth, the centre of the Cornish mining district.

Many were itinerant workers, employed by the Urban Electric Supply Company for the duration of the job, arriving on site after a tramp of twenty or thirty miles. These were not professional 'navvies' but casual labourers, glad to take any job that came their way.

The photograph was taken for the cutting of the first sod, a ceremony performed by Mrs Hanning, the wife of the manager, using a gilded pick. The golden pick may have symbolised the future profits for the directors and shareholders of the Electric Company, for the men, it was a moment's rest in front of the plate camera before the twelve hour a day, back breaking slog of cutting Cornish rock and soil. The wages of the forty men would scarcely have cost the company thirty pounds a week.

'Tommy Atkins being shod by sweated labour' was the slogan of the boot and shoe operatives who marched from Raunds in Northamptonshire to the War Office in 1905. Pressurised by a niggardly Treasury, the War Office bought boots for HM forces at the lowest tendered prices, ignoring a statement of prices drawn up by many of the contractors and the National Union of Boot and Shoe Operatives. The secretary of the Rushden Branch of the Union reported 'work for ankle boots is being given out at a penny a pair for closing the backs and the counters. It takes a good closer ten hours to earn one shilling and she has to find awls and bristles. The statement price for the operation should be two shillings and sixpence a dozen.' The cut price contractors of Raunds resorted to 'basket work', sending the boots out to outlying country districts for finishing.

The union responded by sending two full-time organisers to Raunds, one of whom was the militant socialist, James Gribble. A member of the Social Democratic Federation, Gribble had started work as a finisher at the age of twelve. He had served seven years in the army and saw the best way of winning public sympathy and pressurising the government by leading a march to London. 'General Gribble', as he soon became nicknamed, organised his men on army lines, selecting only one hundred and fifteen of the fittest men from three hundred volunteers.

They set off on 8 May 1905, to the sound of bugles and a band playing 'Rebecca', cyclists leading as an advance guard. Not a man fell out and they received sympathy and practical help all along the route. At Luton, after a triumphant entry, the mayor provided a meat tea and an enthusiastic barber offered to shave all one hundred and fifteen free of charge. Boot blacking manufacturers, Blyth and Pratt, provided breakfast at Watford and so many people gave coppers that they had to be pushed to the bank in a wheelbarrow!

At the War Office, Financial Secretary Bromley-Davenport refused to see them and declared he 'could not see his way fit to interfere between employers and workmen.' Undaunted Gribble made his way to the House of Commons, wearing a

red tie, interrupted a debate from the Strangers' Gallery and was only ejected after a struggle with twelve policemen during which he broke his ankle.

The Social Democratic Federation helped to organise a mass rally in Trafalgar Square where ten thousand gave the strikers a tremendous send-off. Gribble had made history, 'creating an historic precedent in the matter of laying grievances before the highest authorities.' The War Office was obliged to set up an inquiry and agreed that for 1906 and all subsequent contracts the original joint statement with slight revisions would apply.

The strike lasted three months and cost the Union some two thousand pounds. If Gribble was the 'General' surely the hero was John Pearson who was refused permission to march because he was a cripple, nevertheless he marched ahead of the procession all the way to London and back again.

As the Raunds strikers returned from their successful march to the War Office, a great march of the Leicester unemployed prepared to set off to London carrying a message for the king. 'Many of us are old soldiers' read the petition. . . . 'took an active part in the late South African war . . we are reduced to the extreme of misery and want . . . unable to fulfil one of the first duties of husbands and fathers, namely to provide food for our wives and children.'

The march of the four hundred men representing two thousand Leicester unemployed and their families left to a tumultuous farewell from fifty thousand people and a vote by the Leicester Trades Council of thirty-one to twenty-two *against* supporting the march. While a local businessman gave four hundred tablets of soap for washing themselves on the long trek to London, the Trades Council loaned the men their collecting boxes only after the fiercest discussion. The march was to be welcomed in London by the Social Democratic Federation and the Independent Labour Party at a mass meeting in Hyde Park in support of the Unemployed Bill and was opposed by many trade unions because the Bill provided that the unemployed under local authorities should work at less than the union rate for the job.

The men of Leicester were undaunted by the lack of trade union support. Led by the secretary of the unemployed committee, a watchmaker, George ('Sticky') White, the Revd Donaldson and Amos Sherriff they finally committed themselves after months of local agitation to tramping the London Road to see the King.

They had done with passive resistance, the call now was for action. Eight hundred volunteered and half that number were chosen as fit enough for the venture. Spruced for the departure, wearing medals, carrying water bottles and blankets, led by banner and band, they moved off from the packed streets to the tune of 'Lead Kindly Light' on 5 June 1905. The journey was no 'outing', funds were small, the men had been underfed for months and few had footwear to stand the miles of footslogging.

They reached Market Harborough with what a local reporter described as 'poverty-stricken pomp' to a supper of a 1lb. loaf, 2ozs. cheese and a cup of cocoa per man. They washed in cattle troughs filled with fresh water and slept in the cattle sheds on fresh straw.

The journey was continued in persistent soaking rain and by the time they reached Northampton there was an urgent appeal for boots. At Yardley, the local Co-op provided sacks for overcoats, penknives being in great demand for cutting the armholes. On 8 June at Wildchanystead, a local publican was so moved by the plight of one poor fellow that he took off his own boots in the street and gave them to him. Two more days of chilling winds and driving rain saw the marchers in St. Albans, breakfast being bread and butter and tea. By now the men had received a telegram from the Secretary of State for Home Affairs, giving news of the King's refusal to meet them. They reached London on 10 June a ragged army, greeted by Ramsay McDonald asking all on the march to sign the pledge. They spent their first night in the Salvation Army shelter at Burn Street, Edgware, and were given the luxury of a meat tea. The appalling weather washed out the 'great rally' in Hyde Park, a violent thunderstorm scattering them to shelter and ending with the shivering unemployed drying themselves by the furnaces of the St. Pancras dust destructor.

On Whit Monday the weather brightened and so did the men. They marched cheerfully to Parliament Hill Fields, four abreast, a chair was brought from a tea house at the foot of the hill to serve as a platform and the local leaders supported by McDonald for the ILP addressed a crowd of more than six thousand holiday makers. Keir Hardie sent a telegram describing their march as 'heroic', McDonald promised to meet them again and to cheers for London, the ILP and the police they struck off across the heath towards Watford and the road home.

'Lzer, Jinney! Come wenches, you'll ne'er ha' breet een (eyes) if you' lie in bed like that!' This call by a 'knocker-up' was described in Ackworth's *Clog Shop Chronicles*. It would have been echoed by the character in the photograph, taken in Rochdale in 1905 and the mill girls would have dressed for work like the Monday girl, photographed in Rochdale in 1907. The *Chronicles* tell of the work of a 'knocker-up' named Jethro, who 'went his daily rounds with unfailing regularity every morning, except Sunday, between the hours of four and six.' Over his shoulder he carried a long light pole with wire prongs at the end, with which he used to rattle at the bedroom windows of the sleepy factory hands until he received some signal from within that he had been heard. Although employed and paid by the 'hands', Jethro regarded himself as representing the masters' interests, and if a post was unoccupied or a loom 'untended', when the engine started at six o'clock, Jethro felt that it was a reflection on his professional ability and was ashamed and hurt.

This doubtless accounted for the extraordinary zeal which the old man put into his work. The knocker-up was expected to go a second time a few minutes before six to stir up any drowsy person who might have fallen asleep again, and into this second round, which was to many the real signal for rising, Jethro put all his resources. Not only the windows but the doors were assailed, and in addition he would give a word of exhortation in his thin piping voice

> 'Bob! Dust ye'er? It's five minutes to six! Ger up, tha lazy haand (hound). If tha dusn't ger up Aw'll come and poo' thi aat o' bed.'

The practice continued until the Second World War, finally succumbing to the mass produced alarm clock.

SUNDAY

MONDAY

NO 2 COURT

On Monday, 20 November 1905, the Central Workers' Committee had organised a vast demonstration of unemployed to march into the heart of Mayfair.

Assembling that morning on the Embankment, contingents marched in from all parts of the capital. From Islington, Shoreditch, Hackney and Bethnal Green came men led by Dick Greenwood of the Social Democratic Federation and Parson Brooks, the socialist chaplain. Two thousand walked from Hammersmith and Fulham, stopping on the way in Eaton Square to eat sandwiches provided by the SDF. The Woolwich men, some two hundred of them, tramped to Greenwich, crossing the river by steamboat. From Poplar came fifteen hundred organised by the Labour Representation Committee and led by the bewhiskered Lansbury and his two stalwart aldermen, Banks and Sumner. The trade unions supporting the demonstration unfurled their magnificent silken colours of crimson and gold, green and silver, bearing the names of the regiments of the organised working class, The Labourers, General Order, Gasworkers, Riggers, Coal Porters, French Polishers, Machine Rulers and many more. As the march moved away from the Embankment they were led by the banner of the Westminster Unemployed, slogan 'by heavens our rights are worth fighting for'. A Monday afternoon and twelve thousand men headed towards the homes of the wealthy in Berkeley Square. The theme of the protest was carried to the very solid doors of the rich, 'Curse your charity, we want work.' On they went to Hyde Park where twenty thousand heard Jack Williams read a telegram from Keir Hardie urging them 'not to hide in the slums . . . come out and back us in fighting to win the right to work.' The speakers included Harry Gosling and Margaret Bondfield but it was the fiery passion of Jack Williams that had the crowd roaring support as he said 'you have starved too long . . . come out and parade the West End every day.'

On a Sunday in May 1906, the Social Democratic Federation decided to hold a meeting in front of the Market Hall, Nelson. The speakers were Ernest Marklew and Bryan Chapman, secretary of the Nelson branch.

The area in front of the Market Hall was a popular place for speakers, the venue being used by the Salvation Army, the Passive Resisters and the Temperance League. As Chapman started to speak a police inspector accompanied by a sergeant and a number of constables told him he was causing an interference with a public highway. Chapman, standing on a chair, asked the crowd of about three hundred to hold up their hands if they were in favour of the meeting carrying on. They overwhelmingly voted yes. Chapman was arrested and Marklew took his place. Marlkew started to talk on the Education Bill and to the boos and hisses of the crowd, he too was arrested. Supporters gathered outside the police station, only a short distance away and sang socialist songs until they were released at ten o'clock that night.

Chapman and Marklew appeared in court and the Chairman of the Bench, who was also the Conservative mayor said 'meetings are not to be held in the street', fining Chapman ten shillings and Marklew, one pound. Marklew refused to pay. A fierce battle against the police and Council ensued. The police inspector claimed he was carrying out Council bye-laws by keeping the thoroughfare clear. The Council claimed they could not interfere with the police.

Wild scenes followed as Sunday after Sunday thousands packed the centre of the town to hear SDF speakers claim the right of free speech. As one speaker was arrested, another took his place. Marklew was sent to prison for fourteen days. Chapman got seven days. The following Sunday, five thousand marched to the Market Hall led by the Nelson Old Band, singing The Red Flag and led by the banner of the Nelson SDF proclaiming, 'Workers, why talk ye of wages, whose is the wealth of the world but yours?' Arrests and battles followed each Sunday for months and the usual attendance of hundreds for a SDF open air meeting swelled to thousands.

The photograph of Marklew was posed in a studio and sold by the SDF to raise money for the cause.

Middle class onlookers watch as a crowd of unemployed attempt to enter Manchester Cathedral on Sunday, 14 September 1908. Following a meeting of about five hundred of the 'out of work' in Stevenson Square on Sunday morning, they were urged to march to the cathedral by a man called Freewood. Arriving during the litany, the warden forbade entry, but the Dean, Bishop Weldon, appeared and agreed to speak on unemployment if they could come back during the afternoon.

That afternoon nearly three thousand men assembled in Stevenson Square to hear Freewood say 'I want you to demand food and clothes from the people who should be looking after the material and spiritual welfare of the people.' About fifteen hundred then marched to the cathedral, plain clothes police mingling with the marchers and the crowd.

The bishop welcomed them but said it wasn't the province of the church to organise work but if it was necessary to raise a special fund 'many of us will willingly deprive ourselves to aid what is being done.'

The unemployed sat patiently as the vicar of Rochdale preached the sermon dealing with the Prophet Elisha. Then turning to where the men were seated he got as far as saying on unemployment 'I can tell you what the Church can and will do, she will give her sympathy.' At this there was uproar from the hungry men and as the preacher said 'The Church has given. . . . .' Freewood shouted to the sound of prayer books clattering to the floor, 'No, the Church has taken.' The dean stopped the preacher and himself took the pulpit to the cheers of the men and declared the service over. Then leaders of the unemployed leaped over the seats of the pews and began to speak amid great confusion until the cathedral was cleared. The unemployed then reassembled and marched to Walker Street where police drew their batons but failed to disperse them.

The Caslon Letter Foundry was established in 1720 by William Caslon, an engraver of gun-locks from Halesowen, Shropshire. Just how he came to leave the craft he had learned is uncertain, but he was to adapt his skill at working in metal to build such a reputation for his company, that to some his name was synonynmous with Caxton.

Caslon set up his workshop in Chiswell Street, London, and jealously guarded his secret of making the superb metal punches from which each matrix was made. Joseph Jackson, a boy born in Old Street was 'apprenticed to the whole art', but not the cutting of the punches which Caslon and his son worked at alone, locking themselves in a special room. The lad, desirous of learning the mystery, bored a hole in the wainscot and after a deal of diligent spying, applied himself to the art. He presented his first effort to his master expecting praise but received a good blow to the head and a threat to send him to Bridewell, a prison often used for

recalcitrant apprentices. Later, when a journeyman, he was sacked for asking for higher wages.

The firm grew to a considerable size and early in 1900, when this photograph was taken, moved the main works to a purpose-built factory in Rothbury Road, Hackney.

The two boy apprentices on the left are working planers, probably making brass rules of a decorative kind. Notice their coats hanging on nails by the benches, their workmanlike rolled sleeves and the overhead shafting to drive the machines. On a cold morning, the boys would have to give the main belt a pull to help start the machine.

The Caslon craftsman produced work of the highest quality but a complacent management did not heed the development in America of Monotype and Linotype, processes which destroyed a large section of the market for small cast type, and in 1937 the company was wound up.

'Guiness at no time, Warren never, Burrows now' is the slogan on the poster of the Clarion van. The picture was taken during the Haggerston bye-election on 31 July 1908 and shows Miss (La Belle) Maloney, a suffragette leader, speaking for Herbert Burrows, the Socialist candidate. The bye-election, caused by the sudden death of a Lib-Lab MP, was a five day campaign for a safe Liberal seat, complicated by the challenge of Burrows, a pioneer member of the Marxist Social Democratic Federation. A popular figure in East London, he had helped Annie Besant organise the strike of the Bryant and May's match girls in 1888 and was the first treasurer of the Matchmakers' Union.

The women's right to vote issue was a strong factor in the campaign and Warren, a member of the Men's League for Women's Suffrage, had the support of Mary MacArthur's National Union of Women Workers. However, many notable suffragettes, including the Pankhursts and Miss Maloney, were opposed to Warren because he was a supporter of Asquith. The Clarion van was at Haggerston on the day before polling from ten in the morning until eleven at night, provocatively parked outside the Warren campaign headquarters. 'La Belle' managed to draw the crowds away from Warren when he was speaking, politely saying 'I am sure he is a very nice man but don't you vote for him.' Despite a spirited socialist campaign waged under the slogan 'Burrows against Beer and the Bar' a not too subtle play on the brewing interests of Rupert Guiness and the lawyer, Warren, Burrows did not succeed. The final voting figures were Guiness (Conservative) 2,867, Warren (Liberal) 1,724, Burrows (Socialist) 986.

At three thirty on the afternoon of 17 February 1909, the little mining town of West Stanley in Durham was shaken by a dull thud from the colliery that dominated the life and landscape of the community. Within moments a second explosion rocked the mine, flames shooting in an orange spurt, tinged with black over Busty seam leaving a fresh layer of coal dust over the pit head. In those two moments, death reached into almost every home in Stanley, leaving wife without husband, mother without son, brother without brother and child without father.

From the tiny terraced cottages, miners off shift stumbled from their beds and scrambled to the pit, women and children following to stand ankle deep in the mud of the colliery yard over which hung a pall of black dust. A frantic check on the lamp room showed two hundred lamps missing and the sickening awareness of a major catastrophe hit the officials and men on the surface. From the helpless families all eyes were strained with pathetic anxiety toward the shaft of disaster. Their vigil was to drag through the everlasting night as gas flares lit the white and strained faces peering for hope, and hewers queued to volunteer to descend into the abyss of the grim slaughterhouse that was Stanley that night.

John Henry Burn, the owner of the colliery, sent food and, incredibly, champagne to the pit head in readiness for survivors. There were too few to avail themselves of the unaccustomed luxury. Brave men laboured to exhaustion as the first couple were brought alive to the surface to the hopeful cheers of the stricken onlookers. Hours passed and another twenty-four came up, one man having climbed a steel hawser, his hands pierced with the steel threads from his ordeal. The final death toll was one hundred and sixty-three men and boys, victims of firedamp. There were harrowing scenes on the day of the funeral, for scarcely a home had escaped tragedy in the tight-knit community with so many families interlocked in marriage. In Rifle Street, of fourteen cottages, only two escaped death. William Riley left a widow and ten children, the only one of working age a cripple. A little girl wept, her daddy and two brothers had died in the inferno, her mother had died last year. Parents mourned a son of fourteen, he had been found with his hands clasped around the neck of his dead pit pony.

"NED PAGE"
ONE OF THE HEROES OF STANLEY PIT DISASTER.
ALSO RESCUED FROM WINGATE DISASTER.

All was black as at one o'clock the procession moved off in steady drizzle, every blind drawn, eight thousand lining the streets, the lodge banners draped with black crepe, band following band, drums muffled to 'The Death March' as the mourners took five and a half hours to pass. Fifty-nine of the victims were under twenty years of age. The owners sent wreaths.

A relief fund was opened and the lodges levied themselves a shilling a man and sixpence a boy. The local Co-op gave two hundred pounds, the CWS sent a thousand. The owner brothers promised a thousand pounds on condition that the fund was 'clear of creed and politics'. The miners declared that the relief fund should not only be for the benefit of the widows and orphans but *for the men and boys thrown out of work as a result of the explosion.* On the same day as the funeral, two hundred and sixty-seven miners of Mainsforth Colliery were summoned for breach of contract by going on strike for two days. The Conservative magistrate fined them ten shillings each with costs.

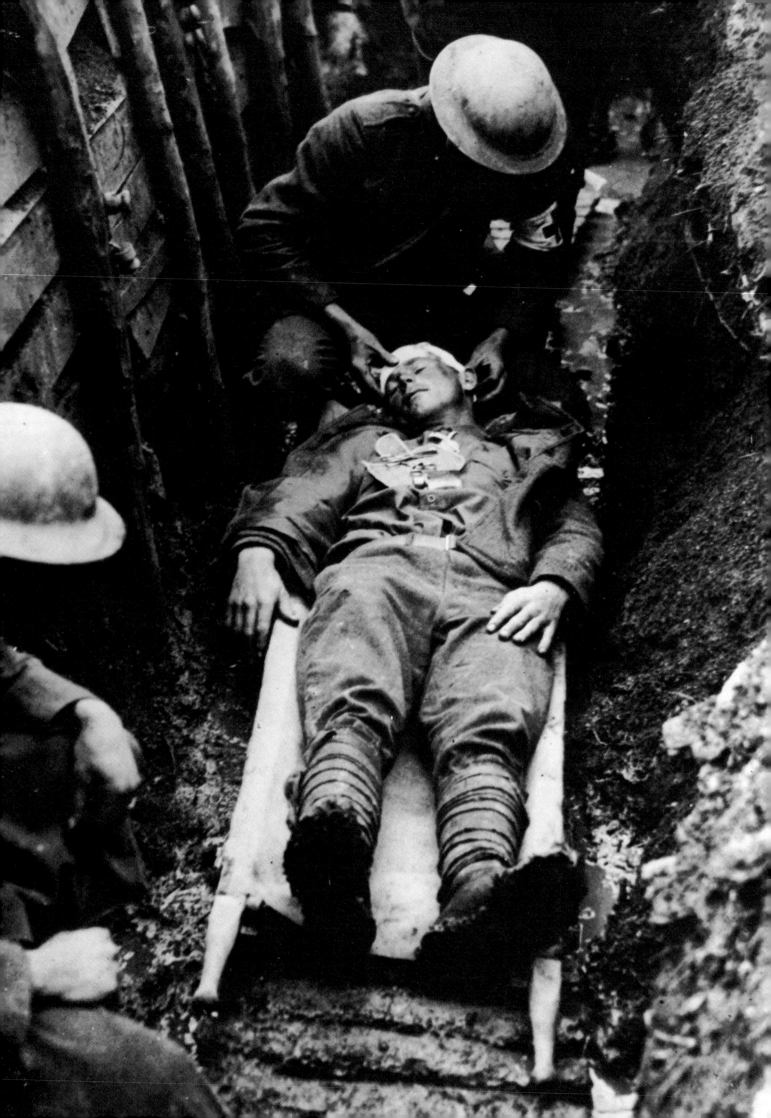

1910

An unknown Durham miner, just in from work, poses for whatever reason, long enough to allow the photographer to leave us with a glimpse of a miner's lot, circa 1910. His home, almost certainly owned by the private coal company that employed him would have faced onto an unmade road. There would have been no garden at the back of the house, just room enough for an earth closet, emptied at intervals by the midden man. Water would have been drawn from a communal standpipe and carried a pail at a time to the house by the women.

Drainage was primitive, being open and filled with filth of every kind. Flies, mice and rats abounded and every summer brought scarlet fever and diphtheria to the children. Inside the house, lit by an oil lamp and candles, conditions would have been as clean as was possible, for the women were slavishly devoted to their housework.

Improvements in sanitation, housing, communications, health and entertainment were almost entirely dependent upon the whim and philanthropy of the mineowners. For the miner there were no holidays, the only prolonged respite from toil being during times of illness, strikes or unemployment. His wage, on which he might have to provide for a wife and a number of children would have been less than two pounds a week.

His real hope for a better future for himself and his family in every aspect of his life lay with the strength of his union, the Durham Miners' Association, representing more than 110,000 at the time the picture was taken.

The story of the founding and growth of the Radcliffe Co-op is not unique, but rather typifies the pioneering enterprise of the early co-operators and their belief in Robert Owen's great discovery that the key to a better society was 'unrestrained co-operation on the part of *all* members for every purpose of social life'. Founded in 1860, the Radcliffe co-operators looked to the established movement in Bury, Oldham and Ashton for inspiration and advice. The founding members would 'cart it' to the towns to attend the tea parties and lectures of the other societies, the strongest contingent of workers coming from the Red Bank Mills. The cut-lookers, overlookers, winders and weavers, encouraged by the obvious success of these societies, soon took the decision to start a Co-operative store in Radcliffe, the first sovereign being subscribed at a pub in Black Lane. Their first meeting was held in August 1860, and incurred them an expense of eleven shillings and sixpence, hire of room costing three shillings, one hundred handbills six shillings, and postage two shillings and sixpence. By October, one hundred and eighty-one workers had subscribed one shilling and sixpence each, enabling the purchase of a flour bin to be made and a shop to be rented in Mount Sion Road for fourteen pounds a year. Stock was ordered, one sack of best flour, five firkins of butter, two flitches of bacon, one box of candles and one sack of soda heading the list. After only one year, the first dividend was paid, two shillings in the pound to each member. The Radcliffe Co-op flourished, reading rooms, educational classes, Women's Guild and political committee interwoven with the steady growth of baking, coal supply, housing, dairy produce and a growing number of branches. Radcliffe was to exist as a separate Society for more than a century, finally merging with Bolton Co-operative in 1963.

Fifty-two boys, each clutching a new sixpence stand before their top-hatted benefactors at a boys' emigration party given by the Lord Mayor of Manchester on 14 April 1910. Culled from the poor law unions of Charlton and Salford, Strangeways gaol and charitable refuges, they passively await departure for their long sea voyage to Canada and their destiny as cheap labour for the farms around Ontario.

While some trade unions reasoned that emigration would lessen the evils of unemployment, some municipalities argued that it would lessen the burden on the ratepayer. As the mayor explained 'the Manchester community benefited economically from emigration. The £12 steerage passage was all that had to be paid for each boy compared with the cost of keeping them for several years.' Thomas Ackroyd, the Hon. Secretary of Refuges, pointed out that they recognised the importance of keeping healthy and honest children at home and preparing them for work in their own country. It was the waifs and strays, the very poor and sickly that

would benefit by being rescued from degrading and dangerous surroundings, saved from a drunken and vicious future and at the same time save Britain from overcrowding. Somewhat in contradiction, he also claimed that it would 'supply the colony with one of their greatest needs, healthy honest labour.'

No doubt many found kindly homes and grew in strength and maturity away from the deathly mills of Lancashire. Others, from the ages of six or seven were bound to work in the fields, putting in a full day's work for no wages, completely in the power of their new masters. The Lord Mayor exhorted the boys 'Be true Britons, true Christians, show your colonial brothers that Manchester boys will do honour to their native city.' Looking at the apprehensive figure of the little lad at the right end of the front row, wearing a charitable overcoat a few sizes too large, you can only speculate as to the effect of those stirring words from the spokesman of the Empire's second city.

Boys' Emigration Party, 1910: Lord Mayor's "Good-bye."

Tom Mann, one of the leaders of the great dock strike of 1889, founder of the militant Workers' Union, the first secretary of the Independent Labour Party, first secretary of the Amalgamated Engineering Union, arrived back in England on 10 May 1910, after eight years of trade union activity in Australia. He was, by that time, a labour leader of international renown with a capacity for appearing at the centre of struggle wherever workers were downtrodden; he was a catalyst for action. He returned from his years abroad, firmly propagating the ideas of syndicalism, industrial unionism, as a means of winning working class power. Within eight weeks of being home he had launched a small publication, *The Industrial Syndicalist*. He wrote 'What is called for? What will have to be the essential conditions for the success of any such movement? *That it should be avowedly and clearly revolutionary in aim and method*.' 'We therefore most certainly favour strikes and we will always do our best to help strikers.' He was not to have long to wait before leading one of the fiercest strikes of the decade.

In accordance with his ideas of industrial unionism, by November he had formed the thirty-six unions organising transport into the National Transport Federation. The first stage of the battle was to be fought against the rich International Shipping Federation who refused to employ any seaman who was a member of the National Sailors' and Firemen's Union. When, in the spring of 1911, every attempt at negotiation had failed, the time came to challenge the owners, the men demanding the right to belong to the union, to wear the union badge, increased pay and an amendment to the conditions of medical inspection to which they were subjected. On 14 June the strike was declared in all the major ports and met with a powerful response. The S.S. *Olympic*, the largest liner built at that time, was due to leave Southampton for New York to bring back American millionaires for the coronation celebrations. The coalies refused to fuel her, the seamen refused to sail her. Within days, the arrogant shipowners who had declined to talk to the union had conceded all the demands.

The lesson of solidarity was clear and in Liverpool on 28 June four thousand dockers came out demanding recognition of the National Union of Dock Labourers and application of union rules at the docks. Seamen, coalies, scalers and carters all followed in support. The strike spread rapidly throughout the city, tramwaymen and railwaymen, the latter against the advice of their leaders in the Amalgamated Society of Railway Servants, joining the struggle. The strike committee met daily, issuing permits for the movement of essential supplies, stopping the carriage of all other goods. The government responded by sending two gun boats up the Mersey opposite Birkenhead, guns trained on Liverpool. Cavalry and infantry with fixed bayonets were drafted in and hundreds of long stout staves ordered for the police. Mann was to write 'Let Churchill do his utmost, his best or his worst, let him order ten times more military to Liverpool, not all the King's horses with all the King's men can take the vessels out of the docks to sea.' On 24 August with all their demands conceded, the strike was called off.

The photographs are two of a single roll of film taken by a professional Liverpool photographer, Carbonara. The eyeball to eyeball confrontation between the sergeant and the striker whilst the young private stares open mouthed at the exchange holds in a moment of time the concept of the unarmed worker challenging state power.

'Your liberty is at stake. All railwaymen must strike at once. The loyalty of each means victory for all.' It was this telegram signed by the general secretaries of the four main railway unions that called the first national rail strike on 18 August 1911. Unrest due to high prices, long hours and petty company tyrannies had resulted in railway workers following the lead of the Liverpool dockers, the men coming out on their own initiative from 23 July. The union executive had jointly asked for negotiations with the railway companies and were met with a firm refusal and a challenge to conflict. 'It is better to have a battle and fight the matter out' said the general manager of a leading railway company to *The Times.*

The Conservative government, before the strike began, assured the private railway companies that they would put at their disposal 'every available soldier in the country'. The Home Secretary was Winston Churchill and he ordered telegrams to be sent to all Chief Constables, informing them that the regulations requiring civil authority requisition for the use of troops was suspended. He passed to the generals the power to decide how, when and where to disperse and use their troops.

58,000 soldiers were mobilised and an inspired commander recalling earlier glories sent the Guards to Waterloo. Sentries with fixed bayonets were ostentatiously placed at main line termini and signal boxes and an army signalling station set up in the Golden Gallery of St. Paul's Cathedral. General Burnley pre-emptively informed the Lord Mayor of Manchester that his troops were marching to the city. The railway companies tried to bribe the men to stay at work, the London Underground offering double pay while the Midland dangled a fifty percent bonus. Despite the inducements 200,000 men came out and within forty-eight hours the government and railway companies in an astonishing volte-face sat down to negotiate with the unions.

It was the massive strike and victory of the London dockers and carmen in August 1911 that seems to have inspired a revolt by women workers in the area of London's dockland. The great transport strike was in its last week during the blazing August sun when a group of women, many of them the daughters of south side dockers, spontaneously walked out of the stifling heat of the confectionary factory where they worked for seven shillings a week (if they were adults, a paltry three shillings if they were girls).

They marched as a group of Pied Pipers, around the Bermondsey factories calling on the women to join them. Out they came, Pearce Duffs', custard powder makers, three hundred girls from Shuttleworths chocolate factory in Southwark Park Road, Sir William Hartley lost his jam makers, Spillers & Bakers, their biscuit makers; to his intense annoyance Sir Thomas Pink saw fifteen hundred of his women workers parade with a banner proclaiming 'We are not white slaves, we are Pink's!' The strike spread to Maconochies' at Millwall, Mortons' preserve factory in Poplar, and Lipton's in City Road.

The action of the women was unpremeditated, they had no trade unions, no strike pay, most of them had husbands and brothers still on strike. The indefatigable Mary MacArthur of the National Federation of Women Workers came to help them and immediately issued an appeal for support: 'many thousands of women are on strike, many more are locked out, the pawnshops are closed and outdoor relief refused. . . . we want at least a thousand loaves at the Labour Institute, Fort Road, by noon on Monday.'

On 14 August fifteen thousand of the women marched, dancing, laughing, singing, brazenly without hats, to a meeting in Southwark Park addressed by Mary MacArthur, Ben Tillett, Dr Salter (later MP for Bermondsey) and Herbert Burrows. Three weeks later, increases in pay had been won at eighteen of the twenty-one factories where the women had struck.

The Mile End Road, South Shields, reeked in the summer months of fish guts and wood smoke, for this was the peak of the herring season and Robertson's were curing. In the small fish factories of the North and South Shields work would continue till midnight and throughout the weekends as women with razor-sharp knives tore the guts from the herring at a speed of hand that would have been the envy of any magician. With toughened fingers and stinging eyes the 'fish girls' worked an average of sixty-four hours a week, for a basic wage of threepence an hour and no extra for evening and weekend work.

In June 1914, the women fish workers of North Shields decided they had gutted fish for long enough at such measly wages, walked out and took the ferry to South Shields. There, one hundred and fifty of them marched from the landing stage to Mile End Road, calling on the workers of Robertson's, Brough's and Fuller's to join them. The response was immediate and enthusiastic, the women from Robertson's, the largest of the fish curers, walked out and persuaded the women workers from Brough's and Fuller's to join them.

The women were not members of a trade union but found energetic support from James Wilson of the National Amalgamated Union of Labour who helped them organise daily meetings at the union offices and at the Spence Assembly Rooms, North Shields. The demands were simple, the women asked for sixpence an hour and overtime pay for evenings and weekends. The employers refused to discuss the matter, a spokesman from

Robertson's calling the demand 'outrageous' and claiming the women averaged twenty-one shillings a week in season and that women worked in the potato fields for one shilling and sixpence a day. Wilson was quick to point out that to earn twenty-one shillings a woman had to work eighty-four hours and that the last wage rise had been in 1887!

The public sympathised with the fish workers and financial support came in donations from the United Women Workers Association and the Harton Lodge of the Durham Miners' Association, both contributing five guineas. The National Union of Railwaymen blacked the handling of fish at the ports and the secretary of the cartmen's union responded to a complaint that his men were moving fish by declaring 'the pen would go through their names in the Society's books.'

Jane Lizzie Townsend emerged as the leader of the women at Robertson's (tallest woman, back to camera) and she borrowed a barrel organ which she and her mates dragged around Shields playing to raise money for the strike fund. This was an act of courage and independence for women at that time and one can only assume that the women drinking in the street are also deliberately expressing their spirit of defiance for such a sight would have been unknown, even in the toughest of the port-side streets.

The strike continued until 4 August 1914, when war was declared and the herring trawlers were commandeered for naval use and fishing ended for the duration.

A classic encapsulation of northern working class life captured by a press photographer covering an unidentified industrial dispute shortly before the war. Clogs, cobbles and shawls are manifest in a street of narrow terraced houses dominated by factories and chimneys. The women and children wait, each with a jug, to collect soup from a communal kitchen, their only hot meal of the day. The 'pinch of poverty' was found pencilled on the back of the photograph, an apt caption applicable to the daily scene in scores of towns at a time when working people never did have butter for tea and would certainly have known the difference had they been fortunate enough to afford the luxury.

Robert Blatchford founded *The Clarion* as a weekly paper in the winter of 1891 to spread the message of socialism. With a combination of wit, warmth and sound political argument the circulation soon reached forty thousand. It became more than a newspaper, it became a movement. Blatchford serialised his *Merrie England* and then issued it as a book selling twenty thousand copies at a shilling each. Wanting to reach out further he issued a penny edition and in less than a year had sold three-quarters of a million. The sales of *The Clarion* reached sixty thousand and Clarion clubs were formed, informally known as The Fellowship. These were followed by the Clarion Cycling Club, joining the new craze with spreading the gospel of socialism to country villages. The supporters of *The Clarion* became known as Clarionettes and in 1895 a few Manchester Clarionettes borrowed a horse and van and set off for Tabley in Cheshire to camp with eight Clarion supporters. The idea of Clarion vans was born. Complete with beds and fitted with socialist literature the vans were mobile propaganda vehicles, touring for weeks at a time. The group posed by the new national Clarion van were photographed at Shrewsbury on 12 April 1914 after a dedication ceremony in the market square. The construction of the van was a socialist enterprise. Designed by the great socialist artist, Walter Crane, Clarionettes made themselves responsible for the enlargement of the Crane panel designs and the glass of the illuminated head. Eight woodcarvers from the Clyde under the supervision of comrade Edmunds carved the nineteen mahogany panels in their spare time for five weeks! The van itself was constructed by a man named Manson at Leith while the collecting boxes were made by Will Hewitt of Harlesden.

The magnificent vehicle was on the road for May Day, launched by the voices of the Potteries' Clarion Choir to journey through Lancashire, in the words of *The Clarion* 'to carry the Clairon message of socialism to the great mass of the workers who live in that benighted district.'

She was to have been the first of a new series of beautiful vans to replace the old ones that had become weather worn after their long journeys around the villages and towns of England, but war was only months away and the photograph may well show the last Clarion van every made.

A strike by building workers at the construction site of the Pearl Insurance offices in Holborn who refused to work with non-union labour was met by the London Master Builders declaring a general lock-out on 24 January 1914. Not content with throwing twenty-four thousand men onto the streets, they insisted that no man would be re-employed unless he signed a statement agreeing to work with non-union labour and sub-contractors. The statement also provided for a twenty shilling fine deductable from wages for any breach of the agreement. This astonishing contract bore a marked similarity to the 'Document' which the building trade employers had tried to enforce during the infancy of the builders' union in 1834. A resolution by the Operative Builders' Society described the new document as 'a challenge to the liberty of combination'.

To the surprise of the employers, even non-unionists refused to sign a document promising not to strike against themselves, and after three months shops and sites remained deserted. Supported by *The Daily Herald,* trade unionists throughout London rallied to give aid and support to the victims of the lock-out and the London Vehicle Workers undertook to provide the men with boots as the dispute dragged through the summer.

The employers reached the stage of threatening a *national* lock-out but the men remained resolute, the struggle for the right of the builders to organise their labour continuing until 4 August 1914 when Britain declared herself at war with Germany.

Britain entered the First World War as the only belligerent relying on a volunteer army. Such was the response to the call to join the colours that the first Military Service Act was not passed until January 1916. If there was any doubt as to whether or not the trades unions and the Labour Party would support the war, the doubt was swept away within a week of the declaration of war in a wave of patriotic fervour. The resolutions of class solidarity, the vows of internationalism, the pledges of strikes to stop wars were as whispers in a wilderness.

On 2nd August only two days before the war, pioneer trade unionist, Will Thorne of the General Labourers' Union, joined Keir Hardie and other labour and trade union leaders in a great anti-war meeting in Trafalgar Square. Long before the war had ended, Thorne became Lieutenant Colonel in the West Ham Volunteers and stumped the country speaking at recruiting meetings. Arthur Henderson was a joint signatory with Keir

Hardie to the manifesto issued by the British section of the International Socialist Bureau, urging workers to combine to conquer the military enemy. . . . 'down with class rule, down with the role of brute force, down with war! Up with the peaceful rule of the people.' But when Ramsay McDonald resigned as Chairman of the Parliamentary Labour Party because of his own opposition to the war, Henderson was ready to take his place.

In his own constituency at Aberdare, Keir Hardie the 'apostle of British socialism' was booed as he declared he 'was going to oppose this war in the interests of civilisation and the class to which he belonged.' These were brave and sincere words, lost in a vortex of hate and a tired and saddened Hardie slowly died as the workers rushed in their hundreds of thousands to join the recruiting queues and enlist for the bloodiest slaughter in the history of man.

The demand of the generals for more and more men to maintain the flow of blood to manure the fields of Flanders inevitably resulted in the depletion of labour available for industry. The answer of the government was the Shells and Fuses Agreement whereby the unions would accept 'dilution of labour' for the duration of the war. In effect, the trade unions were asked to accept the introduction of the twelve hour working day, unlimited subdivision of jobs, the scrapping of apprenticeship agreements and the introduction of unskilled labour in order to produce the hardware of war. Safeguards and rights, painstakingly fought for by trade unionists over a century were to be set aside until the war ended. No similar sacrifice was to be asked of the employers who were to make rich gains by the speeding up of production and the introduction of cheap unskilled labour, the government firmly siding with the employers against the unions. In June 1915 the new coalition government dropped all pretence at negotiation on the question of existing practices in industry and introduced a Munitions of War Bill to force upon the unions the dilution of labour by unskilled men and women.

While many trade union and labour leaders who supported the war acquiesced in the increased exploitation of the working class, other sections began a war of resistance, demanding the rate for the job where new workers were introduced, a control on company profits and a guarantee that the men away at the front would have jobs waiting for them when they returned after the war.

The strongest opposition was led by the Clyde Workers' Committee, a group of shop stewards elected directly from the shop floor under the chairmanship of Willie Gallacher. The Clyde

workers had already conducted a strike for higher pay in February of 1915 and the newly formed committee was more than ready for Lloyd George when he travelled to the Clyde at Christmas of that year as Minister of Munitions to plead the case for dilution as a patriotic duty. Against the advice of his officials, Lloyd George was obliged to meet with the shop stewards and hear out their case for worker control of the factories. At a meeting in St. Andrew's Hall held on Christmas Day, he had the experience of having to stand on the platform while the entire audience got to their feet and sang The Red Flag. Eventually he had to abandon the meeting, the government taking revenge in January by arresting Gallacher, Johnny Muir and Walter Bell on charges of 'attempting to cause mutiny, sedition or disaffection among the civilian population'. The effect of the protest on the Clyde and the continued agitation by women trade unionists did result in 1916 in an amendment to the Munitions Act to give statutory force to 'the rate for the job' where women did the same skilled work as men. Tram, bus and railway companies were forced to pay the rate for the job when the women substituted for men and scores of unions took up the campaign on behalf of women at work.

The unions emerged from the war with an increase of two and a half million members. Women and girls who had been unorganised domestic servants and working class housewives had been introduced to a range of jobs never before open to them and most importantly, they had been brought into the organised trade union movement.

The photographs are of women engineering workers at Manchester and oxide breaking at Beckton Gas Works.

The effects of the war upon food imports and agriculture were not fully felt until the second half of the conflict although rising prices had already effected rationing by purse upon the poorer sections of the community. Eventually the call-up of farm hands, the need for army rations, the restriction of imported food and the shortage of artificial fertilisers combined to force the government to implement a scheme of rationing for the civilian population.

Households were registered, coupons allocated and people selected the retailers with whom they chose to be registered for their rations. Nobody was exempt and it was announced that the king had duly registered with his butcher, presumably Harrods. Bacon and ham were restricted to two ounces a week, butter four ounces and tea two ounces. Horseflesh was allowed at twenty-eight ounces and in a nation with an abundance of horses, delicacies such as 'thin flank of horsemeat' replaced the traditional roast beef.

The first Controller of Food was Lord Devonport, known for his intransigence in dealing with London dockers. The Ministry was installed in the palatial Grosvenor House and the Rubens paintings in the ballroom were covered over so as not to offend the lady typists. When Devonport resigned in 1917 at a time when the shortage of food was becoming a serious problem, Lloyd George sought to placate the increasing discontent of the working class by offering the position to Robert Smillie, President of the Miners' Federation of Great Britain. Smillie declined the uncertain honour and the Prime Minister paradoxically gave the job to the miners' old enemy, Lord Rhondda.

Reduced to the helplessness of a baby in a pram, a wounded soldier is pushed by his compatriots along Granby Street, Leicester, in 1918. By the end of the war, almost three million British troops alone were listed as dead, wounded or missing. The statistics of the conflict, meticulously recorded by the War Office to the very last man and the very last minute of the war, convey nothing of the sheer agonising misery of the limbless, blinded, deformed and shell-shocked survivors of the holocaust of the Western Front.

The war was waged with a contempt for human life on a scale unparalleled in history. General Haig, whose name was to be stamped on billions of artificial poppies, felt that *every step in his plan was taken with divine help* and instructed his infantry to walk at a steady pace, symmetrically aligned, packed in tens of thousands, through the enemy lines. On the first day of the Battle of the Somme in July 1916, sixty thousand young men strolled to destruction. Haig was not deterred and by the time the offensive floundered in the November mud, the British losses had exceeded four hundred thousand in sixteen weeks. King George V promptly promoted the General to the rank of Field Marshall and as the annual summer slaughter was repeated the names of Ypres, Passchendale and Marne became synonymous with stupid butchery.

After the Armistice the higher ranks were rewarded with knight-hoods and peerages while the 'other ranks' returned to stand in the dole queues if they had been lucky enough to survive intact, while the disabled faced the future on pitiful pensions.

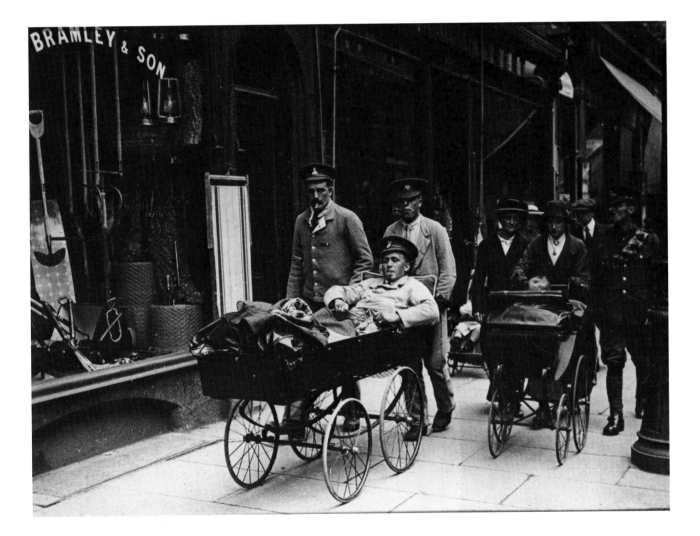

'A pig-killing' was a ritual of necessity, providing cheap food on a communal basis.

People would club together to buy a piglet and share in providing the scraps for making pig swill, nurturing the animal until a suitable size, weight and occasion were reached to slaughter the creature and share in the meat. Alternatively a miner might keep his own pig on his allotment and sell the various cuts, keeping back sufficient for the needs of his own family. Found at Rookhope, Weardale, the photograph shows a group of working men at a pig-killing. The central figure is holding a hammer in readiness for the mortal blow. To his right, a workmate holds an earthenware pot to collect the warm blood to be immediately stirred by his hand until curdled for the making of black pudding. The children, waiting as if for initiation into an adult ceremony, are probably waiting to be given the pig's bladder for use as a football. Not a scrap of the pig would be wasted, from the trotters which would be boiled, to the brains for making into brawn. A miner's daughter described how her father would have buckets of scalding water ready to dowse the carcass enabling the hairs to be removed easily from the skin. 'He would cut the dead pig along the centre of his belly, pull out his innards and fix two stakes across the open body.' Afterwards, the children would run from house to house taking orders for the various parts of the body.

In the mining communities of the North East, leek growing is as much a part of working class culture as the brass band, the lodge banner, the racing pigeon, the whippet and the working men's club. Growing the biggest leek is pursued with the same dedication and passion as the alchemists gave to the making of gold. Indeed, the prize winning leek grower is something of an alchemist himself, feeding his beloved vegetable during the long lonely hours at the allotment with mysterious and secret concoctions of his own making. Bill Williamson who was born at Throckley tells us 'leeks have been fed on beer, urine, blood and human waste. In one case a whole family was barred from the lavatory for a fortnight to provide a good supply of feeding material; in another case, a Northumberland pitman fed his leeks on the scrapings of the baby's nappy, and swore blind that his leeks won because they'd been fed on pure mother's milk.'

The reason for the obsession with leek growing is uncertain. Escape to the allotment and fresh air provide a relaxing and healthy hobby after a shift worked in lung-clogging coal dust in the darkness of the pit. It is cheap and yet can be rewarding in a material way for the competitions offer large prizes as well as the satisfaction of being a champion. The picture of Fred Dawson is posed in the photographer's studio, the leeks placed like holy candles on an altar, trophies carefully displayed, the cup for Fred, the dish for his wife, a compensation for the time he has not shared with her. He stands in Sunday best, with polished boots, flat cap and watch and chain. The writing on the print in unequivocal. The picture of Fred reminds us of the need of people to escape from the monotony of toil, to create, to grow, to build, to make something that is their own.

The children of Tennyson Street Laundry Centre, Clapham, demonstrate the art of scrubbing board, scrubbing brush and mangle. For a working class girl, such training was likely to be an integral part of her schooling to prepare her for her role as a housewife and in all probability, a domestic servant, for even after the Great War there were still more than two million girls and women 'in service'.

For the school-leaver, the prospect of becoming a domestic offered little but enforced independence away from home and a routine of work akin to slavery. Indeed, the girls were nicknamed 'slaveys' or 'skivvies' because of their life of drudgery. Alice Pattinson, a miner's daughter, from Horden, Durham, told how she became a servant girl and described a typical day in her first job. Unemployment in her home area compelled her to seek work away from home and her mother found her a position from a sixpenny agency and put her on a coach to London. Alice was fourteen and had never been away from home or travelled beyond her familiar and friendly mining community. She arrived in London, at the end of a long and tedious journey, sick, tired and terrified, to be met by the master's daughter. The greeting was friendly beyond expectation and she was taken straight to the Strand Palace Hotel for tea, the unaccustomed splendour of which

added to her bewilderment as she struggled to fill her queasy stomach with the only dish she could recognise on the menu, cod's roe on toast. There the fairy story ended.

Her day began at five in the morning when she arose to pump up the bath water for the family; three hundred pumps! After taking up the early morning tea she would clean the fireplace, lay the table for breakfast and then breakfast alone for the only other member of the staff was a child's nurse who dined with the family. Her break over, the endless thread of washing up, sweeping and brushing carpets, preparing vegetables and answering the beck and call of everyone in the house, including the five year old son, wound through her every day, culminating each night in pumping the water again before returning to the box room at eleven at night and crying herself to sleep. Her wage was ten shillings a week and for the first twenty weeks, a shilling a week was deducted to pay back the money advanced for her fare to London. In common with others in her position, she had to pay for her own uniforms, black dress, black woollen stockings, white cuffs and mop hat for mornings and black dress, with white collar and cuffs, smooth stockings, white apron and headband for afternoons. Alice dutifully sent home five shillings a week to her mother to help clear the debt from the clothing club and to help keep the younger children.

The mistress of the house was mean with the food for her slavey and on her one afternoon a week free time, the lonely little girl would spend her time in a tea shop with a plate of doughnuts and a pot of tea. By then, she must have needed it, for on half day she had to rise at four in the morning to do the extra work entailed by her absence. It took Alice three years to save the fare home and when she arrived the village turned out to meet her and hear her tale of life in the capital, for they had never been to London. The four girls on the left were servants in a JP's home near Manchester.

This photograph of an unidentified eviction scene, from the archives of the National Union of Agricultural and Allied Workers, highlights the evil of the tied cottage. Where the farmer was both employer and landlord, the position of the worker tenant was one of near serfdom, bound to his job for fear of losing his home. To join the union, answer back, ask for more wages or a holiday, was to risk dismissal and with the loss of his job went the loss of the cottage. A farmer had the power to dismiss and obtain an order for possession on the slightest whim or pretext. There are cases on record of agricultural workers being evicted for the crime of growing old, their work slowing down after years of service in the fields of farmer and landlord. Others have been evicted after suffering an incapacitating accident while working on their landlord's farm, and in one instance, on a small farm, a claim for arrears of wages resulted in the landworker being turned from his home.

Accounts of the pitiless turning out of the old, the sick and the infirm from their homes, not only by farmers but by mineowners and railway companies, are scattered through the pages of trade union history.

There was an outpouring of platitudes from politicians as the Great War ended with the Armistice of 1918. 'Let us make the victory the motive power to link the old land up in such measure that it will be nearer the sunshine than ever before and that at any rate it will lift up those who have been living in dark places to a plateau where they will get the rays of the sun' proclaimed Lloyd George with eloquence, if without meaning. Tommy and Jack beloved of the fraudulent Bottomley and other war profiteers left the Marne, the Somme, Mons and the high seas to return to a hero's welcome as crosses of stone flowered on the village greens. 'Never again' and 'homes for heroes' fell easily from the tongues of those who had 'kept the home fires burning' while persuading others to do the fighting.

By 1919, the euphoria of victory was tempered with reality as the ex-servicemen returned to the fields and factories to seek their old jobs. The number of trade unionists rose to an unprecedented figure of almost eight million, and thirty-five million days were lost by strikes and lock-outs, the highest figure since 1912 and the second highest since figures were first kept in 1893. Trade unionists in Belfast and Glasgow fought bravely to reduce the working week to help absorb the demobbed servicemen and organisations like the Discharged Soldiers and Sailors' Federation were formed as the post-war boom in trade slumped as quickly as it had soared. As ex-servicemen stood at the kerbs selling matches, playing barrel organs and singing for pennies the number of unemployed rose and by 1921 reached two million.

1920

Fred Gill was not a national labour or trade union leader, but, like so many loyal workers for the cause, quietly and consistently gave his years to the movement and the people he loved. He was a popular man and had one time been Chairman of the Dare Federation Lodge Committee, in the heart of the Rhondda. When he died his comrades (for that was the term used more often than brother among trade unionists in South Wales) wanted to attend his funeral on the afternoon of 13 July 1920 to pay tribute.

The men sent a representative to the management of the Park and Dare pits, offering to start the morning shift an hour earlier so that they would have time to wash and dress in Chapel best before arriving at the funeral. The management of the Ocean Coal Company bluntly refused to allow the men to finish earlier, even though they were prepared to make up the time. So incensed were the miners that they decided as one not to miss the burial of their comrade, but to go to the funeral, straight from the shift.

As work ended, three hundred tramped to Fred's home, assembled and joined the procession. The streets were lined as the begrimed miners, still carrying their blocks, food boxes and tea-jacks, walked in silence to Treorchy cemetery. After the burial they posed before a local photographer to record the heartless act of the colliery management.

One of Fred Gill's last public acts before his illness had been to stand as Labour candidate in the local Council election. His opponent was W. P. Thomas, *Secretary to the Ocean Coal Company.*

THIS PHOTOGRAPH WAS TAKEN AND ISSUED UNDER THE AUSPICES OF THE PARK + DARE LODGES OF THE S.W.M.F. TO COMMEMORATE THE OCCASION OF THE FUNERAL OF COMRADE FRED GILL, HELD UNDER CIRCUMSTANCES WHICH COMPELLED THEIR ATTENDANCE IN WORKING ATTIRE. TEUSDAY JULY 13TH 1920   PHOTO BY C. RICHARDS, TREORCHY

'We care for our widows and orphans' is an old trade union motto to be found emblazoned on many a banner. For the miners in particular, the welfare of the aged is also woven into the history of the miners' unions from the earliest days.

In 1922, when this picture was taken at the offices of the Ashington Lodge, times were hard and desperate even for those fortunate enough to be able-bodied and at work. The effects of the great lock-out of 1921, the Black Friday of the trade union movement, when a million miners went penniless for three months, were still felt in the coalfields. By December 1921, wages had been reduced by up to nine shillings a shift and there were further reductions in 1922. The miners, no matter how hard pressed, were determined that Christmas should bring a little comfort to the old miners and miners' widows of Ashington and arranged a special cash payment for the poorest section of their community.

This was in keeping with the humanitarian tradition of Ashington miners in caring for the aged. Before nationalisation the prospects for a miner upon retirement could be bleak indeed. Most miners lived in a coal company-owned cottage and tenancy was dependent upon employment at the colliery. Retirement often brought evictions and unless there were sons or daughters to provide a home, the reward for a life of work would be the ultimate humiliation of the workhouse and likely separation from the marriage partner. On 17 April 1900, Northumberland miners founded the Northumberland Aged Mineworkers' Homes' Association and Ashington levied each member a shilling as their first contribution. By Christmas 1922, the Association owned 218 cottages, each a dream home in comparison to the deplorable condition of company-owned cottages. Mindful of the needs of the old, the occupants were provided with free coal by the mineworkers of Ashington.

Group of Ashington Miners' Federation Officials
Disposing of Xmas Gifts to Aged People.
1922.

'The Dockers' KC' was an appreciative title won for Ernest Bevin when he argued the case for a sixteen shillings a day minimum wage for dockers and decasualisation of their labour at the Shaw Inquiry in 1920. In answering the dockers' pay claim by electing to put the matter before a public court of inquiry, the employers imagined they had the advantage, briefing the formidable Sir Lynden Macassey KC, an experienced counsel in industrial cases, to overawe and outwit the working class witnesses who would appear for the union.

Bevin, a thirty-nine year old national organiser of the Dockers' Union with James Sexton to assist him, was given the task of putting the case for the Transport Federation. His performance was brilliant. Though lacking in formal education he spoke for eleven hours, vividly describing the history, work, poverty and danger of a docker's life and scoring heavily in exchanges with the Chairman of the Port of London Authority, the wealthy Lord Devonport, an old enemy of the dock workers.

While the two sides were involved in academic argument as to whether or not a docker and his family could live on the employers' proposed wage of three pounds thirteen shillings and sixpence a week, Bevin went shopping in Canning Town. That evening he prepared a 'docker's breakfast' and took the plates into court. When Professor Bowley, the employers' expert witness, went into the box, calculating the precise number of calories on which a man could live and work, Bevin pushed scraps of bacon, bread and fish before him and asked the Cambridge professor if that was sufficient for a man who had to carry heavy sacks of grain all day. The witness protested. 'You have never carried 2cwt. bags on your back continuously for eight hours?' fired Bevin. 'No' replied the professor. Bevin then produced a menu from the Savoy Hotel and asked him to calculate the calories in a shipowner's lunch! The outcome of the inquiry was a triumph for Bevin, the court condemning the system of casual labour and awarding a national minimum of sixteen shillings a day for a 44 hour week.

Was it fair, reasonable or even possible that the poor should keep the poor? It was hardly equitable that a rich borough such as Westminster, where a penny rate raised more than thirty thousand pounds, maintained only eleven hundred on outdoor relief, while Poplar, where a penny rate raised only three thousand pounds had to maintain forty-four thousand. The East End of London as a whole, with only a quarter of the paying capacity of the West End, had seventeen times the liability.

In March 1921, Poplar, blighted with mass unemployment, casual dock labour, rotten housing and slum landlords, reached breaking point. Faced with a massive increase in the rate, a burden the poor could not carry, the Council refused to cut the level of relief to the unemployed and decided not to pay £270,000 due to the central authority, the London County Council, carrying a rate of four shillings and fourpence in the pound, to meet the needs of the Council and the Board of Guardians.

This was the essence of the conflict that was to lead to the imprisonment of the mayor and the majority of the socialist members of the Council and the introduction of a new word into the English language, 'Poplarism'.

Summoned to appear at the High Court on 29 July the Council marched in procession from Bow with the mace bearer at their head, the mayor wearing his chain of office and all beneath a banner saying 'Poplar Borough Council marching to the High Court and possibly to prison'. Following the councillors, who included the stalwarts John Scurr, Charlie Sumner, Charlie Key, Edgar Lansbury and his father, the 'uncrowned King of the East End' the kindly George Lansbury, came the people of Poplar,

trade union banners fluttering in the summer breeze, to give support to their elected representatives. The court ordered payment, the Councillors refused and in September, nearly all the Council was sent to prison for contempt. Fifteen thousand marched to Holloway, many of the women carrying babies in their arms, as Minnie Lansbury, Susan Lawrence, Nellie Cressall, Julia Scurr and Jennie Mackay were taken away.

While Herbert Morrison deplored their actions and J. H. Thomas called the councillors wastrels, the fight continued even inside the prison. The Poplar Borough Council demanded and won the right to hold a Council meeting in Brixton Prison, the women members being brought from Holloway to attend. Outside, ten thousand enrolled in the Tenants' Defence League and pledged to refuse to pay rent if the councillors asked. Faced with the resolution of the Poplar councillors and their enormous support from the electorate, the High Court released them in October so that they could attend a conference to discuss the whole matter. The result was a victory for Poplar. The Council had made their first charge the care of the sick, orphaned, aged, widowed, workless and homeless and forced the introduction of a Bill equalising rate burdens between the rich and poor.

The photographs are taken from an album presented to Councillor C. E. Sumner at a meeting of the Council held in the Council offices on 9 November 1922. Each councillor who had been imprisoned received a copy. The caption to the picture of Poplar women carrying loaves given by the Guardians is entitled 'Give us this day our daily bread' while the other photograph shows Alderman Hopwood 'surrounded by his bodyguard'.

Charabanc day trips were a popular working class leisure activity during the 1920s and the elected representatives of the trade union movement enjoyed them as much as their members. The 1923 Trades Union Congress was held at Plymouth under the chairmanship of J. B. Williams of the Musicians' Union. Perhaps as an escape from the worrying discussion at Congress on the financial plight of *The Daily Herald,* the General Council decided to take a charabanc outing to Dartmoor, chugging along at a maximum of twelve miles an hour.

For the sharp eyed, the bearded man in a cap is Ben Turner of the Textile Workers and the group at the rear of the first charabanc, from left to right, are A. B. Swales, AEU, A. Conley, Tailors and Garment Workers, A. Purcell, Furniture Trades, H. Gosling, Watermen and Lightermen, W. Thorne, General Workers' and R. T. Jones, Quarrymen. The capped figure in the front may be Walter Citrine. Other identifiable figures include J. Varley, Workers' Union, E. L. Poulton, Boot and Shoe Operatives, H. Skinner, Typographical Association and J. Bowen of the Post Office Workers.

Charabanc pictures from the early twenties are common and others found included the annual outing of the workers from scores of factories including Falmouth Gas Works and the refuse destruction workers from Walthamstow on a jaunt to Epping Forest.

The outing of the Norland Ward Women's Group of the North Kensington Labour Party could easily be mistaken for the Kensington Conservative and Unionist Association were it not for the identifying placard and *The Daily Herald.* The woman on the left in the front row is taking the Party's red flag and most of the group are wearing red rosettes. The substantial looking Labour Club proclaims Socialism and Recreation and the women decked in their prettiest dresses have no doubt earned the break from shop, factory, housework and local canvassing for the party. The photograph was taken by J. B. Vere, a professional photographer from Notting Hill, who claimed by rubber stamp on the back of the photograph that his terms were 'very moderate'.

Alice Pattinson, the daughter of a miner from Horden, Durham, found these photographs a mirror of her own memories of life in a miner's cottage during the twenties and thirties. Her grandmother had five boys, 'all in the pit', and because they worked on different shifts was tied to a treadmill of endless toil to feed and care for her sons. Working between them, the fore-shift (5 a.m. to 1 p.m.), the back-shift (1 p.m. to 9 p.m.) and the night-shift (9 p.m. to 5 a.m.), her grandmother never found time to go to bed, but slept at intervals in a rocking chair by the fire. As each shift ended she had to boil water in the copper in readiness to fill the tin bath in front of the fire. The hot water would be carried by her in an enamel bowl to the bath and the men would kneel beside it, washing away the coal dust from all but their backs. In her village, the miners left the coal on their backs to toughen the skin and in the belief that it strengthened their backs. Alice recalls that when her father was working a narrow seam his back would be raw, as though he had been whipped. During the enforced leisure of the 1926 lock-out, the miners would play other workers at football, they wore no shirts and the miners teams were easily recognisable by their black backs.

While her father bathed, Alice would 'dash' his pit clothes, banging them against the yard wall to remove the loose dust and

then hang them to dry. He often worked up to his knees in water, with water dripping in from above, wearing only his 'hoggers' (short trousers). At the end of a shift of back-aching toil he was faced with a three-mile walk home, often in driving rain or freezing sleet. The fire in the range was always 'happed up' and the clothes would be draped on the backs of chairs in front of the fire and hung from a line across the mantelpiece. In some of the cottages, there was a brass rail fitted across as seen in the picture of the miner bathing. On Thursday nights, her mother would let the fire die out to clear all the dead ash and clean the range. The range would be blackleaded, the fire bricks whitened and the back of the chimney polished with blacklead as high as the arm would reach. The brass fender would be shone, the poker polished and ashpan burnished and for a few hours, the altar of family life would be as she loved it to be, spotless.

All the cooking would be done on the fire and in the ovens of the range, with working class ingenuity stretching the meagre pay to provide appetising and nourishing food. 'Panackalty' was a favourite dish made of layers of potato, onion and corned beef covered with Oxo gravy. Other dishes would be leeks fried with bacon, a thick broth made from soaked peas, bacon and stock and thick stew with barley and dumplings.

The life of a miner was hard, but the life of a miner's wife was no less so, if devoid of the danger. The daily round of unremitting housework, childbearing and providing and caring for the men, husband and sons, on wages that at the best of the good times were never meant to give more than subsistence, took a physical toll. Alice tells that her grandmother, at the age of fifty-four, one day said she was tired and would lie down for while. In an hour she was dead. The doctor said she was not ill, simply worn out.

In 1926, the school leaving age was fourteen, though many left at thirteen plus and boys were legally allowed to work underground in mines at the age of fourteen, to enter the most dangerous industrial occupation in the country. The statistics were simple. Every five hours a miner was killed. Every working day, 850 suffered injury. Every ten minutes, 5 were maimed. In the three years from 1922 to 1924, 597,198 miners were injured and *no records were kept for those off work for less than seven days.* Combined with work that was physically destructive over a long period, productive of diseases such as pneumonconiosis and silicosis were working conditions that are virtually indescribable and company-owned housing that was some of the worst in Britain. The reward for labouring beneath the earth varied from eight shillings and fivepence a day in South Staffordshire to ten shillings and ninepence in South Wales.

The mineowners were joined together in a powerful employers' organisation known as the Mining Association. They represented such owners as Lord Londonderry, the Duke of Northumberland and Lord Gainford, men whose interests extended to banking and ownership of the press. They also spoke for the landed gentry, aristocrats like the Duke of Hamilton and Lord Bate who drew royalties on every shovelful of coal sweated and hacked from beneath the ducal sod, both drawing more than £100,000 a year from their 'rights'. It was against this background that the Mining Association, strongly supported by the government of Baldwin, Churchill and Hicks, combined to demand that the miners work longer hours for less pay and stated that the mines would be closed to all who did not accept the new conditions from 2 May 1926.

The message from the owners was clear; never again would they meet with the miners' representatives, never again submit to national agreements but insist on district agreements to break the power and unity of the Miners' Federation of Great Britain and force down the living standards of the miners to an even lower level. The smallest reduction would be imposed on mine labourers in Scotland, eightpence farthing a day, the largest on hewers in Durham, three shillings and eightpence a day.

A. J. Cook, the fiery secretary of the MFGB replied 'We are going to be slaves no longer and our men will starve before they accept a reduction in wages.' His words were prophetic.

As early as 26 February the TUC had reiterated support for the miners, declaring 'there was to be no reduction in wages, no increase in working hours, and no interference with the principle on national agreements.' In the face of the impending lock-out a special Conference of Executive Committees of the unions met at the Memorial Hall in Farringdon Street on Thursday, 29 April, and continued in session until Saturday, 1 May. By that time, the miners had been locked out since midnight on 30 April.

The decision to call a General Strike in support of the miners was taken at midday on Saturday, May Day, 1926 by 3,653,527 votes to 49,911. Telegrams were sent out on 4 May and more than three million workers came out on strike.

The photograph of a local agitator taken in a northern mining town at the start of the strike depicts a scene repeated throughout the country as strikers held spontaneous local meetings in support of the TUC. What the speaker is telling his audience, we shall never know, but all over the land was repeated the slogan coined by Cook, 'not a penny off the pay, not a minute on the day'. The picture shows in great detail some aspects of the period in a north-eastern mining community; notice the boy and some men wearing clogs, the wide cloth caps and one man in his Sunday best bowler, the miner holding his pigeon basket, the neckscarves and the small brick backyards of the houses.

'We look upon your "yes" as meaning that you have placed your all on the altar of this great movement and having placed it there, even if every penny goes, if every asset goes, history will ultimately write up that it was a magnificent generation that was prepared to do it rather than see the miners driven down like slaves.' With this passionate statement, Ernest Bevin left the delegates at the Memorial Hall on 2 May 1926 to organise the biggest strike of workers in British history.

The General Councils' call had not been for a total strike of all organised workers, but a first attack by the front line industries. Transport and railwaymen, who with the miners constituted the old triple alliance, dockers, printing workers, iron and steel trades, chemical and power workers. The response was overwhelming. As intelligence reports poured into the TUC headquarters at Eccleston Square (a house once owned by Winston Churchill) from the Trades Councils, the message was clear, the strike was solid in defence of the brave miners. The immediate and loyal response of the local organisations in support of the strike took both sides by surprise. Unlike the government that had been actively planning for the confrontation since July 1925, the trade unions had made few preparations, hoping that the strike alone would force the owners and government to withdraw their demands for a cut in wages and longer hours and to negotiate a settlement.

It was left to local trade unionists to form Councils of Action, Strike Committees and Emergency Committees to control the movement of goods, disseminate information to counter government propaganda, arrange strike payments and organise demonstrations and activities in support of the strike. The photograph of trade unionists marching in support of the strike at Leamington Spa is typical of thousands of similar popular demonstrations of solidarity that took place throughout Britain. Though the establishment feared revolution, the march of building workers and railwaymen has the air of a nineteenth century trade union procession, the carpenters and joiners parading examples of their work, window sashes and door frames, through the streets on the back of a horse-drawn wagon. The figure marked with a cross is E. Horley, a member of the Bricklayers' Union.

At Methil, in Scotland, the trade unionists reacted to the call in a highly organised manner, the Trades and Labour Council forming itself into a Council of Action with sub-committees for food and transport, information and propaganda and mobilising three cars, one hundred motor cycles and countless bicycles for its courier service. Speakers were sent out in threes, a miner, a railwayman and a docker to emphasise the spirit of unity with the miners. Later in the strike the Council of Action added an entertainments committee and more seriously a Workers' Defence Corps after some savage baton charges by police upon the pickets.

The snapshots are from Methil, one showing miners and their families waiting to hear speeches from local leaders (one man sitting on the grass is holding a bugle used to summon the people from their homes).

The other shows pickets arrested during disturbances at Muiredge (left to right, Grory, Williamson and Munro).

Soup kitchens were familiar enough during the depression years between the World Wars and reached a peak during the lock-out and General Strike of 1926. There were two kinds of kitchens in operation, those organised and funded by well-meaning groups of citizens and the communal kitchens supplied and administered by the miners themselves.

The first photograph shows women and children queuing at the Hippodrome Music Hall Theatre, Rotherham, during the strike, for the allowance of one ladleful of soup and one slice of bread per person. This kitchen was one of more than thirty set up in Rotherham during the strike and was administered, as were most of the others in the town, by the Salvation Army. Most of those receiving soup collected it in enamel jugs, though all sorts of utensils were used to carry away the warming liquid, including mugs and saucepans. The names of strikers' dependants were carefully listed and each family was allocated a specific kitchen.Ellis Hibbert, the son of a striking steelworker, recalling the soup kitchens in Rotherham, remembers being sent to collect his allowance from the basement of a large house in Tusmore Street, not far from the Hippodrome. The soups were mainly vegetable in composition and Hibbert particularly remembers pea soup, but does not recall there being any meat.

The second photograph, from Yorkshire, shows a sympathetic shopkeeper handing out bread to miners' children. Help from small local shopkeepers by granting credit and making gifts of food was common in the close-knit mining communities but with a few exceptions, big business was more concerned with feeding undergraduate strike breakers.

Government plans to cope with the strike of the Triple Alliance of miners, railwaymen and transport workers, or for a general strike originated in 1919. The TUC seemed unaware of the government plans to distribute supplies by road though Lloyd George claimed that Ramsay McDonald was aware of it and even prepared to make use of it during 1924. The organisation had evolved steadily during a period of continued industrial unrest and was accelerated after 'Red Friday' in 1925 so that the government was not only ready to take on the miners, but was looking forward to dealing the unions a massive blow.

A network of Civil Commissioners was established in September 1925 which read like a cross between Debretts and the Services List. The system included military liaison officers as well as police representatives, with headquarters in Whitehall. One hundred and fifty road officers were appointed who gathered support from the private haulage industry. One committee operated from Cadby Hall, using the gratuitous services of J. Lyons for distributing food, while other industrialists in the distributive trades like James Paterson of Carter Paterson, the hauliers, and Mr Rudd, a well-known meat haulier, also joined the committee.

At the same time, private support for a strikebreaking force came from a body calling itself the Organisation for the Maintenance of Supplies under the leadership of Lord Hardinge of Penshurst.Other committee members included Admiral of the Fleet, Lord Jellicoe, and General Sir Francis Lloyd. The professional classes hastened to enroll and the inaugural meeting of the Sheffield OMS gives a fair indication of the types who volunteered. The chairman was the Chairman of the Sheffield Conservative Federation and *The Sheffield Telegraph* and Hon. Colonel of the 71st Field Brigade of the Royal Artillery. The vice-chairman was a director of four companies and Lieutenant Colonel of the 4th West Riding Brigade. The managing director of John Brown steelworks was on the committee as was Sheffield's Economic League representative.

The armed forces were strategically stationed, armoured cars and tanks brought out for guard and escort duties, the Riot Act read to the troops and even artillerymen were given bayonet drill. The photograph shows troops carrying an ammunition box into their temporary quarters at the Tower of London, where incidentally the contents of London's gunshops were stored during the strike.

Since 1925, the number of special constables had been increased from 98,000 to 226,000 and a special reserve had been created. The number was increased by 50,000 during the strike by reliable volunteers from the universities, the professions and by retired army officers who happily donned the blue and white armband over cricket sweaters or Fair Isle jumpers and drew their truncheons and steel helmets from the government stores. The class divisions were clearly drawn and while for the most part it was a question of answering a patriotic call, for many it was a chance to 'teach the blighters a lesson'. Swaggering polo playing ex-officers wielded yard-long clubs and flourished whips as they cantered in military formation in Hyde Park replete with jodhpurs and Empire builders' helmets.

In a strike remarkable for a lack of violence, given all the ingredients for near civil war, it was the specials who were involved in some of the most brutal incidents during the nine days. Mounted specials supported the Black and Tans in an unprovoked attack on a mixed crowd in Lewes Road, Brighton, while at Bridgeton attacks by the specials on unoffending citizens led to an official protest by the Glasgow Town Council Labour Group. Specials took part in raids on trade union offices and arrested workers for selling strike bulletins; for the miners it was a fight for survival, for the university students and their middle-aged fathers in search of glory, it was all jolly good fun.

The rail unions met with an almost hundred percent response to their strike call in support of the miners, on the London, Midland and Scottish, the largest of the four main railways, only 207 out of more than 15,000 drivers reported for work. This presented the plus-four brigade of strikebreakers with an adventure straight from the pages of *Boys' Own Paper*, the chance to be an engine driver. For some, the chance included one of the most prestigious and romantic of all British engines, *The Flying Scotsman.*

In the tiny village of Cramlington on 10 May 1926, a meeting of the Cramlington Lodge was held at the Miners' Institute. One of the officials ended the meeting with A. J. Cook's stirring appeal, 'Stop the wheels turning'. Later that day a group of the miners saw some blackleg platelayers working on the rail lines at Cramlington and they stoned them and chased them away. One of the miners said 'come on lads, let's have a rail out' with the intention of pre-venting any blackleg coal trains from passing. Another of the group was posted on the bank four hundred yards down line to warn any approaching train to stop, while some of the others forced open a rail hut and took sledge hammers for knocking out the blocks. Twenty or more lifted out the rail and waited for the coal train to approach. To their astonishment, *The Flying Scotsman,* with a strikebreaking crew of volunteers, slowly drove to the section where the rail had been removed and gently toppled over. Fortunately because of the warning given the train had slowed to less than 20 m.p.h. and nobody was hurt.

The derailment of *The Flying Scotsman* was a national sensation and a police investigation began at once. Eventually a miner, Lionel Waugh, whose brother was a policeman and whose uncle was a police inspector, betrayed his comrades, turning King's Evidence. Nine miners were arrested and given sentences of four, six and eight year's penal servitude.

Comrades, victory! This was how a trade union official announced the news of the end of the General Strike to a mass meeting of workers at Gravesend. With the strike solid and growing daily, with spirits high and trades councils in calm control of many areas, the ending of the strike was interpreted in hundreds of towns and villages as a triumph for the miners. As the truth slowly became known of the unconditional surrender of the TUC to the government, the news was received with shock and disbelief. 'Surrender of the revolutionaries' crowed *The Daily Mail,* 'Surrender received by Premier' cried Churchill's *British Gazette.* Only Bevin of the TUC deputation to Baldwin sought an assurance against retribution. None was given. 'Thousands will be victimised as a result of this day's work' was Bevin's comment on the meeting.

The first to act were the railway companies, turning away railwaymen who reported for work, victimising loyal workers who had given decades of service. The NUR was forced to sign a humiliating document that included the words 'the trade unions admit that in calling a strike they committed a wrongful act.' The coal owners seized the opportunity to exclude militants from the pits, refusing to engage those whose names appeared on their blacklists. Many miners were refused work for years and in one instance a blacklisted miner was not re-employed until 1939 when Britain went to war.

The Conservatives, high on victory, introduced an Act of Parliament making General Strikes illegal and attempting to sever the financial link between the unions and the Labour Party. It was made a punishable crime for a worker in 'essential employment' to commit a breach of contract; in effect, a return to the old law of master and servant, swept away by the Employers' and Workmen's Act of 1875.

Such was the level of Tory vindictiveness that on the eve of a visit by a delegation of British miners to the United States for financial aid, Baldwin sent a letter to the US authorities stating that there was no dire need in the British coalfields.

With the sad return to work of the three million solidarity strikers, the miners were left, not to fight a bloody battle, not to rally for a glorious attack, but to attempt to survive a lone, long weary struggle of attrition against a merciless Conservative government. The miners were precluded by the Poor Law from receiving relief in an act directly attributable to coal owners. The Powell Duffryn Steam Coal Company had brought an action against the Guardians of Merthyr Tydfil for giving poor relief to miners in the 1898 strike and the Court of Appeal had issued a definitive judgement that stated Guardians may not give relief to able-bodied men on strike for whom work was available. The government was quick to insist that work was available (albeit for longer hours than established by Act of Parliament and for lower pay than the previous agreement between the mineowners and mineworkers) and demanded that the law concerning relief should be vigorously applied. It was left for the dependants of the miners, their wives and children, to claim relief at the starvation level of five shillings for a wife and two shillings for each child. At the beginning of the dispute some Poor Law Unions relieved the pit boys aged fourteen to sixteen because under the Trade Union Act of 1876, they were not allowed to join a trade union and therefore had no say in the dispute. Devoid of any pity, the Law Lords in July stated that the fact of not being able to vote did not affect the Merthyr Tydfil judgement and they were subsequently debarred from relief. More than four million British citizens were faced with the severest deprivation and the gloating Cabinet was to utilise every law on the statute book and even to introduce a special new law, the Board of Guardians (Default) Bill, in order to rule by hunger.

How then were the miners able to exist for nearly seven months before being driven to accept the terms of the owners? The answer lies in a spirit of community struggle, of a feeling of 'We're all in it' in the fight against a common enemy. It was a spirit not to be felt again in Britain until the blitz on London in 1940. The mining communities were under siege.

Aid for the miners and their families came from the organised labour and trade union movement, but with four million mouths to feed it was, at its best, dropping crumbs into a bottomless stomach. The General and Municipal Workers gave twenty thousand pounds, the Weavers' Association ten thousand. Collections were taken, levies volunteered, loans made. Russian trade unionists collected and sent just over a million pounds, a magnificent gesture of solidarity but equal to only five shillings for each dependant. Co-ops extended credit in the form of food vouchers, gave away free bread and made long term loans. The funds of the miners' unions were hopelessly inadequate. The Durham Miners' Federation was able to make only two payments of ten shillings each to its members and the seven payments from the MFGB amounted to three of five shillings, one of four shillings and three of three shillings.

As the plight of the miners grew worse the government continued to apply pressure to the siege. In June, they sent an official note of protest to the Soviet Government in an effort to stop the collections of money for the miners. In July, they announced that a Bill would be passed lengthening the working day in the mines. Throughout the country Tory ratepayers protested at the payment of relief to the miners' wives and children. Lord Askwith, President of the Citizens' Union, incorporating the Middle Classes' Union, urged the Minister 'to direct the Boards of Guardians to cease granting relief to the dependants of miners and others in places where the pits are open.'

In the mining villages, communal kitchens were opened to provide one meal a day and food was wheedled from local farmers and shopkeepers to pop in the pot. (The photograph shows George Hurst, MP, at Low Valley, Darfield, tasting soup made by miners' wives.) For the men, existence drifted to tea or cocoa and bread and marge, the margarine being concocted from a paste made from turnips. Occasionally assistance came from unexpected sources, a firm of Newcastle bakers giving a thousand loaves a week for

South Shields and Sunderland, Fry's of Bristol sent seven thousand five hundred tins of cocoa. These were the high spots, as the weeks became months, the communal soup was fortified with dumplings made only from flour and water.

The miners scavenged the beaches and hillsides for coal, driftwood and small trees to use as fuel. Coal picking and outcropping were not without hazard for the police often arrested for stealing and the cutting of drifts into the hillsides was as dangerous as mining ever is. The photograph of miners at Cheadle with their primitive 104 working gives an idea of the precarious character of the activity (p. *130*).

Relief days were organised and fancy dress bands and glee clubs toured to entertain and raise money. In the picture of miners in fancy dress, one is wearing a German helmet, a souvenir from the war. Miniature miners' lamps were sold by the thousand at a shilling each and the proceeds of A. J. Cook's own account of the strike, *The Nine Days,* went to the miners' wives and children fund.

The allotments, so loved by miners as an escape into the daylight world were worked as never before. Rods and nets were brought out for the catching of fish for personal consumption or for sale at threepence a pound for the relief fund for children. Bread was distributed to the children, bought with the money raised, as seen in the photograph of loaves being given out from the working men's club in Middle Street, Barnsley. Rabbits were poached, the odd sheep rustled and potato fields raided as Neville Chamberlain instructed the authorities to tighten up on relief payments. In the end, with winter impending, the miners were beaten by starvation and the owners and their agents checked their blacklists and carefully selected those they would choose to re-employ. The hardship and bitterness lingered on, the memory and folk memory surviving in mining towns and villages to this day. In December 1926, W. P. Richardson of the Durham miners said in an interview 'The miners are on the bottom and have been compelled to accept dictated and unjust terms. The miners will rise again and will remember because they cannot forget. The victors of today will live to regret their unjust treatment of the miners.'

William Gibson Hodgman gave a lifetime of selfless service to the labour movement. Born in 1893 he left school at the age of thirteen and after taking a few odd jobs became apprenticed as a shipwright at Irvine's Harbour Yard in Hartlepool in 1908. He joined the Associated Shipwrights' Society and remained a proud member all his working life.

Bill Hodgman fought his first trade union battle while still an apprentice, insisting on the full rate for the job at twenty-one years of age although his seven year apprenticeship did not finish until he was twenty-two. To the delight of his fellow apprentices the management conceded his claims and his life as a militant trade unionist had begun.

Moving to Rosyth to work at the naval base, he organised a rent strike against the authorities who were charging eleven shillings a week for rent for housing on the estate. The strike lasted three months and ended in victory for the tenants, the rent being reduced to six shillings a week. While at Rosyth, Bill Hodgman represented the Shipwrights on the Clyde Workers' Committee and in 1918 joined the Independent Labour Party. He returned to Hartlepool where he organised classes in economics in conjunction with the Central Labour College and was prominent in the great unemployed struggles in Plymouth during the twenties and thirties. On May Day, 1920, Bill Hodgman (fourth from left, second row) along with a group of trade unionists and their families were invited aboard the first Soviet ship to dock at Hartlepool after the Revolution. The banner reads 'Long Live May 1st. The International Holiday of the Toilers, 1920. Proletarians of All Lands Unite!'

Nicola Sacco and Bartolome Vanzetti were Italian immigrants to the United States. They were also anarchists. Accused of armed robbery and the killing of a security guard, their case became a *cause celebre*, joining together such diverse figures as Stalin and Mussolini in pleading to the US President to spare their lives. They were gentle idealists, who, because they were radical and alien, were easy victims of hate and hysteria. The prosecuting attorney described them as 'regular Wops', whilst Judge Webster said of Vanzetti 'although he may not have actually committed the crime attributed to him is nevertheless morally culpable because he is the enemy of our existing institutions.'

The photograph shows one of the twelve cars used by the International Class War Prisoners' Aid Association to rally support for a mass meeting held in Hyde Park. Twenty thousand answered the call and heard George Hicks (Chairman of the TUC), A. J. Cook and Wal Hannington condemn the proposed judicial murder. Despite world-wide appeals for clemency Sacco and Vanzetti were burned to death in the electric chair on 23 August 1927. 'Give 'em the juice' said the Revd Billy Sunday.

Bartolome Vanzetti's final letter remains as an eloquent testament to their martyrdom. 'If it had not been for these things, I might have lived out my life talking at street corners to scorning men. I might have died, unmarked, unknown, a failure. This is our career and our triumph. Never in our full life could we hope to do such work for tolerance, for justice, for man's understanding of man as now we do by accident. Our words—our lives—our pains—nothing. The taking of our lives—lives of a good shoemaker and a poor fish peddlar—all. That last moment belongs to us—the agony is our triumph.'

With only one and a half million workers receiving a single week's holiday with pay at the beginning of the twenties, a day at the seaside was the extent of the annual break enjoyed by the majority of families. Charabancs, as they were still called, provided the means of escape from mill or factory to popular resorts like Blackpool and Southend and 'trippers' brought joy to some and misery to others. 'No charas' signs hung at some pubs and cafes while others welcomed them with open tills.

Those who could afford a week away, mainly the young marrieds and the highly skilled workers, went off by train or charabanc to stay at Balmoral, Blenheim or Chatsworth; not the stately homes but the seaside boarding houses that boasted such grand names. Those who found good 'digs' might return year after year to the rough pleasure of cold linoleum, high teas and low prices. In Lancashire, the cotton mills closed for Wakes Week and local papers carried details of the amounts paid by mill holiday clubs and gave the numbers of trains and charabancs leaving for excursions to the coastal resorts. In the good times, when work had been steady, almost half the population of a mill town might leave between midnight on Friday and midnight Saturday at the start of Wakes Week. If the holiday meant sleeping on the sands and changing into a damp costume beneath a raincoat, who cared, you were with your mates and it was better than working.

The photograph was taken at Burnley coach station in the late twenties and shows workers leaving for a Wakes Week holiday.

The Daily Herald was launched on 25 January 1911 by a group of journeymen printers, locked out for demanding a forty-eight hour week. The first issue sold 13,000 copies and sales grew but the paper did not survive the dispute and collapsed after thirteen weeks. The efforts of the printworkers in producing *The Herald* were not wasted, for they had shown that there was a sale for a trade union paper. In 1912, Ben Tillett of the dockers' Union, T. E. Naylor of the London Compositors, C. W. Bowerman of the TUC and George Lansbury raised a small sum and on 15 April revived *The Daily Herald* with a mere £300 left in the kitty. Although Lansbury was not named as editor until 1913, it was Lansbury's *Herald*. Despite many vicissitudes, the circulation fluctuating wildly between 50,000 and 100,000 and the bailiffs appearing at the office more than once, the paper won tremendous loyalty from staff and readers. Uncompromisingly socialist, it was a paper for rebels, supporting strikes, opposing wars, providing a platform for suffragists and syndicalists and offering a public gallery for the brilliant cartoonist, Will Dyson.

The First World War effectively killed that kind of *Daily Herald*. The paper, under the pacifist editorship of Lansbury could not compete with the war stories provided by the capitalist press and avidly sought by the public. By September 1914, the paper appeared only as a weekly.

There was a resurgence of the paper in 1919, with financial support from the trade union and Co-operative societies but it continued to struggle and in 1922, Ernie Bevin led the TUC and Labour Party into joint ownership and in 1925, Lansbury quietly resigned.

The photograph of women supporters of *The Daily Herald* was taken at Reading by Arthur Lovegrove in 1929. By then, McDonald was Prime Minister of the first majority Labour government and Odhams Press held fifty-one percent of the shares in the paper.

'The Women's Red Army marching through East London to Epping Forest, 1928' reads the pencilled inscription on the back of this rare shot of the LLX, the women's section of the Labour League of Ex-servicemen. The women and some men, about two hundred in all, had assembled at Gardiner's Corner in the East End and marched through Mile End, Bow and Stratford, held a rousing meeting at Leytonstone and continued onwards to Epping Forest, closely followed by plain clothes officers of the Special Branch.

On practising their marching in a forest glade, an urgent message produced the arrival by car of the Commissioner of Police who accused them of performing military movements. Apparently they succeeded in convincing the Commissioner that they were only practising their marching in readiness for May Day and the police withdrew, leaving the 'red army' to dance on the greensward and make their way back by bus, having been forbidden to march. The uniform was first seen in public on Sunday 11 March 1928 when thirty-five women, led by Mrs J. R. Campbell marched into Trafalgar Square for an International Women's Day meeting and took up a position on the plinth, along with the speakers who included A. J. Cook, Majorie Pollitt, Beth Turner and Hanna Ludewig from Germany. The uniform was officially described as 'fawn coloured blouse and serviceable short skirt, stockings to match, flat-heeled brown walking shoes, khaki berets, red tie and regulation armband'.

An official Communist Party pamphlet described the LLX as having 'guarded the plinth' and it would seem that they and the uniformed men drew their inspiration from the Workers' Guard in Germany where the Red Front Fighters numbered some three hundred thousand.

The Prince of Wales became the Patron of the National Council of Social Services in 1928, a charitable organisation dabbling with the problems of unemployment. That year, he made an extensive tour of the depressed areas in South Wales, Tyneside, Scotland and Lancashire (where he is pictured shaking hands with a worker at Middleton) meeting men who had been unemployed for years. He seemed sincerely and visibly shaken and is reported to have said 'Some of the things I see in these gloomy, poverty stricken areas made me almost ashamed to be an Englishman. . . . isn't it awful that I can do nothing for them but make them smile.'

Eight years later after his accession to the throne, he made his noted tour of South Wales to witness the effects of a decade of capitalist slump in the Rhondda and Monmouth valleys. After being shown the derelict steel works at Dowlais, that once provided employment for nine thousand, he uttered the words that are remembered to this day 'something must be done to find them work.' Desperate and hungry men and women grasped at the hope offered by the words of their monarch but the young MP for Ebbw Vale, Aneurin Bevan, was furious. 'To organise an expedition to Wales as if it were an unknown, barbarous and distant land, much in the same way as you might go to the Congo' was an outrage. He said that the king was being used to mask persecution and that Ernest Brown, the Minister of Labour who accompanied the king, was the instrument of that persecution. He declined a suggestion that he should meet the king at Rhymney, saying 'I cannot associate myself with a visit which would appear to support the notion that private charity has made, or can ever make, a contribution of any value to the solution of the problem of South Wales.'

It took a world war to bring work to South Wales and by then, the Prince of Wales, alias Edward VIII, alias the Duke of Windsor, was leading the life of a useless aristocrat in another land.

1930

The bleak 1930 April scene at Ferryhill in the north-east coalfield is a misty memory of humble and poor men seeking the right to work. The lone figure on the soap-box addressing the bleak assembly is George Cole, local miners' leader and militant trade unionist. The small contingent with banners and rucksacks are the north-east section of the unemployed march to London, on their way to join another thousand from Scotland, Northumberland, Plymouth, Yorkshire, Lancashire, Nottinghamshire, Derbyshire, Staffordshire, the Midlands and Kent. The first march of the unemployed in the thirties, it was a small demonstration compared with the great marches of the twenties and the even greater processions of unemployed to follow over the rest of the decade. The factor that gave it a special significance was that it was the first protest of the workless directed at a *Labour government.*
The march was organised by the National Unemployed Workers' Movement (inaugurated on 15 April 1921 at the International Socialist Club, Hoxton) and it divided the loyalties of Labour supporters and met with bitter hostility from official Labour bodies. Northampton Labour Party said 'we cannot support a movement in opposition to the government.' Nevertheless the McDonald government had failed to halt the steadily increasing number of jobless and in fact unemployment had increased from 1,169,000 when Labour came to power in June 1929, to 1,770,000 by May 1930. Surviving all attempts to hinder their progress, the marchers arrived in London on May Day, to be greeted by twenty thousand at the entrance to Hyde Park, with another thirty thousand at the meeting inside. That night the weary marchers presented themselves at the Fulham workhouse, refused to be treated as casuals, won the right to beds and food (cooked under the supervision of the Marchers' Control Council) and to the fury and astonishment of the Workhouse Master, hoisted the red flag over their quarters.

The General Election of 1931 was one of misery for the Labour Party as they fought the most divisive contest in the history of the movement. Elected in 1929 for the first time as the largest party in Parliament, the government had floundered in a quagmire of capitalist remedies for world capitalist slump. Pledged to solve the problem of unemployment, the newly appointed Minister for Unemployment, J. H. Thomas, had boasted 'I have the cure' as he hob-nobbed with bankers and watched the number of registered unemployed soar from 1,163,000 on taking office to 2,500,000 within eighteen months. Wal Hannington, the Communist leader of the workless, was to sarcastically remark that 'as Minister of the Unemployed, J. H. Thomas is a howling success.' As the government pursued the traditional Conservative remedy for recession by cutting expenditure and wages, the TUC Economic Committee warned in March 1931, 'the application of such a policy can only intensify the slump by reducing the purchasing power of the community thereby leading to further unemployment.' The Cabinet preferred the advice of Sir George May, former Secretary of the Prudential Insurance Company and Sir Montague Norman, Governor of the Bank of England—cut expenditure by £96,000,000 and effect two-thirds of that sum by reducing maintenance for the unemployed by twenty percent. Bevin and Citrine led a trade union delegation to a Cabinet Committee and declared total hostility to the cuts. Sidney Webb, who was a Secretary of State in the Cabinet, said to his wife, Beatrice, 'the General Council are pigs, they won't agree to any cuts of unemployment insurance benefits, or salaries, or wages.' McDonald led a traitorous caucus, including Snowden and Thomas, in forming a National Government with the Liberals and Conservatives and the election was a straight fight between the Labour Party and other parties in office led by McDonald. In an atmosphere of monetary panic, Labour representation in the house was cut from 289 to 46. Ernie Bevin (left in photo) contested the safe seat of Gateshead (Labour majority 16,700) and lost to the National Liberal, T. Magnay, by 12,938 votes.

A strong Yorkshire cricket team, including star players, Bill Bowes, Hedley Verity and Emmot Robinson took the field to play a scratch London team in a fund-raising match for Manor House Hospital early in the 1930s. Played at Walpole Park, Ealing, the London team also included some notable performers, albeit some of them were footballers, and were ably captained by the irrepressible 'Patsy' Hendren of Middlesex and England. The outcome of the match is not recorded in the pages of *Wisden*, but Reginald Silk, a London photographer, has left us with this record of the teams.

The Manor House Hospital grew from 'The Allies' Hospital Benevolent Society' founded during the First World War by voluntary contributions, for the treatment of wounded soldiers. The war over, the hospital turned to caring for the casualties of the industrial battlefield, accident victims from the mines, quarries, ships, factories and docks. Established as a Friendly Society, the hospital is owned by the Industrial Orthopaedic Society and receives over ninety percent of its funds from the subscriptions of its members, who for the most part are workers in British industry. The hospital since its inception has enjoyed a special relationship with the trade union movement and a number of unions make an annual donation to the hospital in addition to the support given by individual members.

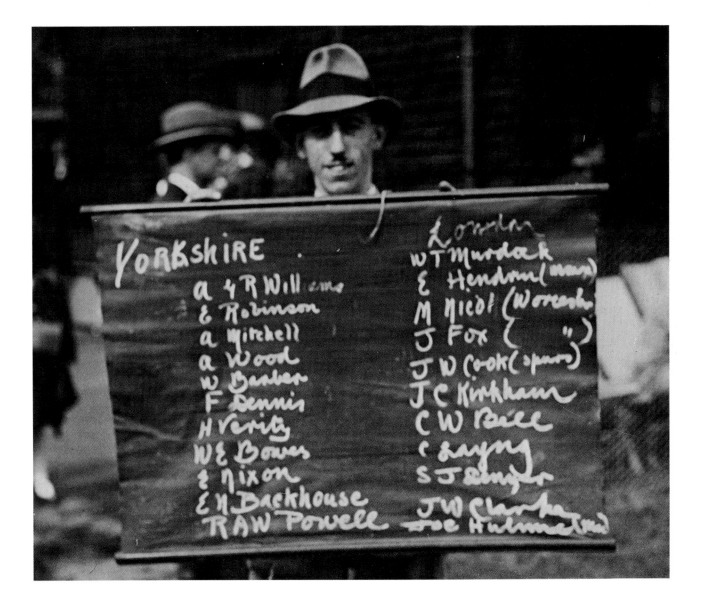

The National Unemployed Workers' Movement organised a nationwide march against the means test policy of the National Government in the autumn of 1932, unemployed workers marching on the capital from as far afield as Scotland and Plymouth.

Throughout the year, the unemployed had continued to demonstrate against the cuts and inhuman conditions of the National Economies Act, imposed by the National Government led by Ramsay McDonald. The cuts had reduced the rate of adult benefit from seventeen shillings a week to fifteen shillings and threepence for men and from fifteen shillings to thirteen shillings and sixpence a week for women with corresponding reductions for younger applicants. A second decree had increased the number of claimants falling within the conditions of the new means test to 825,000, subjecting millions to the humiliation and degradation of inquisition by the government means test investigators. By January 1932 the registered unemployed had soared past the 2,500,000 figure and 1,143,025 were in receipt of poor relief. It is significantly recorded that 15,795 persons entered the casual wards as tramps that year, a social tragedy that was to provide cartoonists with a new source of material for decades to come. People were poverty-stricken by the million, deprived, helpless and frustrated. From time to time they fought back with mass fury, directing their anger towards the officials at local and government level who operated the unfeeling machinery of state. The Territorials were called out to guard the Town Hall in West Ham, 15,000 battled in Bristol and 10,000 held a running fight with the police in North Shields as they tried to reach the Public Assistance offices. County Hall and Parliament were the scenes of fierce fighting between police and unemployed in London. In Birkenhead, following a peaceful protest of 10,000, police clubbed the dispersing crowds, beating down men, women and children and then going on a night long rampage of terror, through working class streets, breaking windows with their truncheons, dragging

men from their beds and beating them bloody in front of their wives and children. In Belfast, the fighting with the police reached such proportions that the Royal Inniskilling Fusiliers equipped with machine-guns were drafted into the city, martial law was imposed and the troops fired on the workers, killing two and wounding scores. When veteran trade unionist Tom Mann went to Belfast to attend the funeral of Samuel Baxter, one of the victims, he was arrested at the gates of the cemetery and returned to England.

It was against this background that the 2,500 marchers tramped for miles in cold and rain, slogged the cobbles, slept in workhouses and were cheered by workers through every town and village. In Wakefield, thousands turned out to greet the contingent of forty women marchers. In Lancashire, a fishmonger gave the marchers a free fish and chip supper, workmen threw Woodbines and took off their own coats and scarves to give to the marchers and Co-op cobblers mended boots without charge.

In London, they arrived to a tumultuous greeting from 100,000 assembled in Hyde Park and to a police welcome from the batons of the 'specials'. On 1 November the marchers planned to take a petition of protest, bearing a million signatures, to the House of Commons. On that day, the police arrested their leader, Wal Hannington, raided the NUWM offices without a warrant, removed five hundredweight of documents and that evening broke up the demonstration in the West End and confiscated the petition.

Later in a lawsuit, the NUWM represented by Sir Stafford Cripps, KC, D. N. Pritt, KC, and G. R. Mitchison, successfully sued Lord Trenchard, the Chief Commissioner of Police, winning damages and costs and the return of their property.

The photographs show Wal Hannington and Harry McShane leading the Scottish marchers and contingents from Teeside and Sunderland crossing the Tyne Bridge.

Keeping the unemployed from engaging in undesirable activities, like marching, demonstrating and demanding work or full maintenance became the concern of a wide section of the employed middle class during the years of depression.

Here, at Bootle in January 1933, a group of unemployed are seen quietly making mats at the Bootle Services Club. Local businessmen, retired army officers and Rotarians rallied to keep the men off the streets by contriving to create useful work, albeit unpaid, by providing premises and raw materials. The mats were made from rope taken from the heart of the great ropes formerly used to moor transatlantic liners. Soaked for years in sea salt, the rope acquired great strength and the finished mats promised a lifetime of use. No money was paid for the work but the men were allowed to keep the articles they made for use in their own homes. Other activities to occupy the unemployed in the area included casual work on the land, pea picking and potato lifting. Such was the lasting and seemingly permanent state of unemployment that the local men actually had their own football team, the 'Bootle Unemployed'.

To their credit, the Oldham Public Assistance Committee passed a resolution refusing to administer the means test, though they were forced to give way by the Ministry of Labour who threatened that such a refusal would result in the whole of the cost of relieving applicants having to be paid from local funds.

Wiredrawers withdrew their labour and their tools from the factory of Richard Johnson & Nephew Ltd, Manchester, in June 1934.

The dispute originated much earlier, in June 1932, when the company invited Charles E. Bedaux Ltd., American efficiency experts, to visit their works and 'give some idea of the cost of achieving economies.' The time and motion study engineers duly arrived and by November of that year, despite considerable misgivings from the men, the Bedaux system was being operated in the stranding shop. For two years the Amalgamated Society of Wire Drawers and Kindred Workers negotiated, issued statements and reasoned with an obdurate management as wages were reduced and work speeded up. In February 1933, the company, with considerable effrontery and in consultation with Bedaux, put forward a proposal for the union and the state to subsidise the increased profitability of the firm. In every three weeks, two weeks would be worked and unemployment insurance from union and government drawn for one week!

Against a background of nationwide unemployment, the men with immense courage and total solidarity resisted the erosion of their job security and deterioration of working conditions, challenging the right of employers to measure their lives to a fraction of a second. Finally, the strike was precipitated in the cleaning shop, a key department where sixteen men faced a double shift reorganisation leading to a cut in wages of seven shillings and sixpence per week. As the Bedaux man walked through the door, stopwatch in hand, the men stopped work. They were no longer prepared to be 'watched and beset'. The sixteen, all 'old servants' of the firm, were dismissed with due notice and in response five hundred men struck work immediately in support of the sixteen.

The men who walked out were, for the most part, local born men from Bradford, Beswick, Openshaw and Gorton, skilled workers, long serving, not the sort to be hasty in judgement. The strike lasted nine months and was not officially ended for two years, racking a local community with misery, the pawnshop and poverty as scab labour from outside the area was brought under police protection to the Johnson works.

The strike was not won. Men were victimised. A year after the strike had started a thirty-eight year old man was told he would never work for the company again. He entered the kitchen of his house, sat down, told his wife and with head in hands, cried. He got his next job two weeks before war broke out in September 1939, after six years without work.

The national hunger march of 1934 was marked by the restraint and discipline of the marchers in spite of police harassment and attempts by the government to treat the protestors as potential rioters. Although the march, organised, as most of the great hunger marches of the thirties were, by the National Unemployed Workers' Movement, did not have official support from the Labour Party or the TUC, rank and file support was substantial. Local Labour Parties, trade union branches and Co-ops gave practical help and encouragement to the protest and risked the wrath of their executives. The Independent Labour Party granted John McGovern, MP, leave to march with the five hundred strong Scots contingent and agreed that McGovern should present a petition to Parliament requesting permission for four of the marchers to be heard at the bar of the House to put their case for the withdrawal of the Unemployment Bill.

The marchers came from all the major areas affected by mass unemployment, from Cornwall to Fife, leaving weeks before their planned arrival in London on 25 February. A feature of the march was a women's column drawn from various areas and representative of unemployed women and wives of unemployed men from a variety of trades and towns. The women assembled at Derby for their wintry pilgrimage and the picture shows some of them receiving foot treatment during the trek.

The photograph of women being waited on at table was one of the more pleasant breaks on the route and was specially provided by a local Co-op. The tea-chest picture is of a meal break, hot food previously prepared being taken from a hay-box. Billy cans of hot food packed in hay would remain hot for hours enabling the marchers to enjoy a hot meal on their stops between towns.

As the marchers steadily made their way in bitterly cold and wet weather along the roads and through the towns, gathering strength, the Home Secretary, Sir John Gilmour, launched the first attack to discredit the hunger marchers, stating 'the

government will have to ask Parliament to grant such powers as experience might show to be necessary to deal with such demonstrations.' The threat was clear and two days later, the Attorney-General, Sir Thomas Inskip, speaking at a meeting, warned of bloodshed and said the government would be bound to take steps to stop it. Petty police harassment followed the contingents all the way; at Birmingham where the marchers spent the night in the workhouse, the police stayed with them in the sleeping quarters claiming they were there in case of fire! After McGovern and McShane had finally persuaded the superindendent to withdraw the police at midnight, a large number of police were discovered hiding in a room upstairs and the superintendent pretended he did not know they were there!

As the marchers drew close to London, the clamour from the establishment for suppression and restriction increased. The Duchess of Atholl asked the Home Secretary if he would take suitable steps to prevent the hunger marchers from holding meeetings in Trafalgar Square. The Tyneside contingent was visited by police and five marchers arrested for 'wife desertion'. This action was instigated by the public assistance authorities because their wives were claiming poor relief. The men were later to prove that their wives supported them in marching and that the authorities were merely creating difficulties.

It was the attempt of the government to brand and condemn the hunger marchers before they reached London that led to a number of prominent men and women forming a committee to maintain a vigilant observation on proceedings, taking the name Council of Civil Liberties. Signatories included C. R. Attlee, H. G. Wells, Kingsley Martin, Ellen Wilkinson, A. P. Herbert and D. N. Pritt. By 23 February the contingents were drawn up around London in readiness for their entry and reception at a great rally in Hyde Park on Sunday 25. The Home Secretary ordered the call-up of ten thousand special constables and provincial police were also drafted in to support the Metropolitan force. McShane and Jones repre-

senting the Scots and Welsh marchers met a hundred MPs at a special meeting in the House of Commons and won warm support for their request that some of the marchers should be heard in the House. In the meantime, the March Council requested a meeting with the Premier, Ramsay McDonald, in a letter signed by Aneurin Bevan, James Maxton, John McGovern, Tom Mann, Ellen Wilkinson, Harry Pollitt, Wal Hannington, Alex Gossip, James Carmichael, John Aplin, John Figgins and Maud Brown. In conjunction with the march, a national congress was held at Battersea Town Hall, attended by nearly one thousand five hundred delegates, representing three-quarters of a million workers. The delegates were welcomed by the Mayor of Bermondsey and at the same time informed that Harry Pollitt and Tom Mann had been arrested on the charges of making seditious speeches in the Rhondda the previous week. As Pollitt was to have taken the chair at the congress and Mann to have moved the main

resolutions, it could be construed that the authorities had not relented in their policy of harassment.

In drizzle and intermittent heavy rain the hunger marchers finally made a footsore entry into Hyde Park, where, despite the inclement weather an estimated one hundred thousand people gathered around eight platforms to hear the speakers and pay tribute to the courage of the hungry emissaries from the valleys, towns and highlands of Britain. Packs on their backs, complete with first-aid wagons and field kitchens, the marchers were cheered through the surging crowds, greeted by the waving banners of the Labour League of Youth, Co-op guilds, trade union branches and trades councils.

The marchers did not succeed in putting their case to the House although they were supported by a large number of MPs and had the support of Sir Herbert Samuel, leader of the Liberal opposition. Clement Attlee spoke for the marchers, saying 'The marchers

are fair representatives of the unemployed. The injustice from which these men and women suffer is very widely known in all parts of the House and the feeling in the country is now tremendous . . . . there is no reason why these men should be refused a hearing by the cabinet.'

The marchers sent a deputation to Downing Street, led by Maxton, McGovern, McShane and Hannington. McDonald was not at home. In the Commons, McDonald in an outburst said. . . . 'has anybody who cares to come to London, either on foot or in first class carriages, the constitutional right to demand to see me, to take up my time whether I like it or not? I say he has nothing of the kind!'

It was left to the workers of London to give the true response to the hunger marchers at a great rally on Sunday 3 March in Trafalgar Square. Crowds gathered along the route from Hyde Park to the Square as the hunger marchers had a last meal from their field kitchens and proudly marched, singing The Red Flag to an overwhelming reception in the Square. The picture taken in Trafalgar Square shows all heads turned as a section of the audience see the approach of the unemployed. A collection was made to send the two thousand men home by train and thousands gathered at the main line stations to see them on their way. At Kings Cross, the Scots contingent were all wearing red rosettes and waving red handkerchiefs as they were cheered from the station. In Glasgow, people lined the streets six deep to greet their safe return and twenty thousand packed Enoch Square to welcome them home.

If the national government was unmoved, the marchers had won enormous public acclaim and support for their refusal to starve in silence.

On 1 March 1935, Alderman John Coupe, JP, the Conservative mayor of Stockport travelled to St. James's Palace, London, to meet the Prince of Wales. The purpose of his visit was to join other lord mayors, mayors and chairmen of Urban District Councils to discuss with the prince plans for the Jubilee of King George V.

The Finance Committee of the Stockport Corporation made provision for the expenditure of three thousand pounds on the celebration which included the presentation of eighteen thousand mugs bearing the portraits of Their Majesties, one to each school-child in the area. Stockport at that time had eight thousand workless and the decision to lavish three thousand pounds on royal junketing while so many lived on the very edge of starvation brought an immediate outcry from the unemployed. The expenditure seemed even more outrageous in the face of the implementation of part two of the 1934 Act which brought many of the unemployed into the new scheme of the Unemployment Assistance Board, cutting payment for a married couple from twenty-six shillings a week to twenty-four shillings, on the very day that their mayor went to meet the prince. To compound the plight of those out of work was the decision of the Council to cut the rates by threepence in the pound, reducing the money available for public work which might have offered jobs to some of the unemployed.

Alderman F. Bowler, the leader of the local Labour Party, led a protest march to the Town Hall on 6 March and some of those that took part in the demonstration are seen wearing their placards of protest. The men formed a cordon around the Town Hall and Bowler pledged to fight inside the Council against the rate

reduction and for more jobs. The Labour group put down a motion urging the Council to 'respond to the Prince of Wales' appeal to employers to engage an extra one percent more men on permanent employment' arguing that they should be used on public work for the benefit of the town.

The Council rejected the idea and proceeded to prepare for a banquet in the Town Hall (11 May), to floodlight the public buildings, illuminate a horse from the cleansing department and fire a salute of twenty guns.

To placate the hungry they offered a half-crown voucher on application to the borough treasurer's office to registered unemployed and old age pensioners. In an act of incredible parsimony they excluded any OAP's in receipt of public assistance! To match their meanness the Chamber of Trade recommended a public holiday to mark the Jubilee, leaving it to

the employers to decide whether or not to pay their workers. As a result, only one mill gave the day off with pay, thousands of workers celebrating the Jubilee with a reduced pay packet.

The king in his speech was obliged by the government to make reference to the unemployed, saying 'I grieve to think of the numbers of my people who are still without work.'

All over Britain the workers decorated their houses and streets and made the most of the occasion with a spirit that must have dismayed true socialists. The people of Salford danced to gramophone music in the streets while Londoners provided sit-down teas in the streets for the children. In Fleet Street, Communists pulled a stunt when a banner stretched across the road bearing a loyal greeting, changed at the pull of a string to read 'Glorious reign, unemployment, hunger and war'.

Then rouse to our tread
When you hear us marching by
For servility is dead
And the means test too, must die

These words sung by the hunger marchers reverberated throughout the country as the marchers took to the roads from eleven different cities on the last and the largest of the great thirties protests against unemployment, the means test and the policy of the National Government towards the workless. This time the marchers were part of a united demonstration embracing all sections of the labour movement and they marched strengthened by the organisation and help of the Trades Councils and the constituency Labour Parties.

Public opinion against the wickedness of the principle of means testing families was at a peak. The iniquitous and petty economies of the government that brought acrimony and family division to the tables of the poor were hated by all but the self-satisfied Tories who had never enjoyed the experience of bureaucratic inquisition. A worker with a new born child would claim the allowance, to be asked 'is the child being breast fed?' If the answer was yes, benefit was refused. A fourteen year old boy might get a job as cheap labour while his father remained unemployed, the boy's earnings were counted and the family benefit cut, for the boy should keep his father. In Merthyr where unemployment reached nearly sixty percent of the population, nine thousand people, more than seventy percent of the unemployed, were on means test, for unemployment had lasted for years. Mothers went without food to feed their children while the children went without boots, for there was not enough money for food and boots. In the winter months, coal was bought four pennyworth at a time as families struggled to exist on means tested allowances. So contemptuous were the government to the workless that when Mannie Shinwell, MP for Seaham, tabled a resolution asking the Prime Minister to meet representatives of the marchers, the Tories walked out of the House.

By contrast, public response to the marchers was magnificent. The Lancashire contingent were given a twelve mile bus ride paid for by Oxford students. When the eight hundred marchers from South Wales, carrying their Keir Hardie banner from Aberdare, reached Slough, they were greeted by eleven thousand, for Slough was a little Wales, peopled by those who had fled the valleys of death. At Lincoln, the marchers were met by the rural Dean and the Sheriff, at Newport, welcomed by the Crosskeys Silver Band. Hailed and fed by Trades Councils and Co-ops along the way, the hunger marchers were in good spirits for their triumphful march into the capital where a quarter of a million turned out to acclaim the men the government treated as human scrap. The photograph shows some of the Welsh marchers lining up outside Cater Street School, Camberwell, where they had spent to night, prior to the march to the Hyde Park rally. Thousands lined the streets with clenched fist salutes and packed around the six platforms set up in the park to hear the speeches of Will Thorne, MP, James Griffiths, MP, C. W. Gibson, Chairman LCC, Arthur Horner, President South Wales Miners' Federation, Aneurin Bevan, MP, Clement Attlee, MP, and many more, putting the case the government did not want to hear.

As the autumn leaves drifted across the banners, Attlee moved the resolution . . . . 'the scales (of unemployment benefit) are insufficient to meet the bare physical needs of the unemployed. . .' and winter was ahead.

In the midst of mass unemployment, trade depression and crippling poverty, the private landlords continued to exact a terrible tribute from the working class. The conditions in which the majority of industrial and agricultural workers lived were appalling, crammed into delapidated houses that were breeding grounds of pestilence. The slums of Liverpool, Glasgow, Manchester and London ranked with the worst in the world and the landlords had first call on the wages of the workers, exacting an average of twenty percent of their income, always enforcible by the power of eviction.

In the London Boroughs of St. Pancras, Holborn, Finsbury, Shoreditch, Bethnal Green, Poplar, Bermondsey and Southwark 400,000 were living more than two to a room. In Shoreditch alone, 100,000 people were existing in one square mile. Workers lived in nineteenth century tenements, sharing lavatories and taps. Baths in working class houses were virtually unknown. Others lived in basement flats, in a world of perpetual twilight while those fortunate enough to live in a terraced house invariably took in lodgers in order to meet the rent or shared the house with married sons or daughters. In 1930, the medical officer of Hammersmith told of a man with a wife and four children living in three rooms, his income forty-five shillings a week, his rent £1. In St. Pancras where wages were nearer fifty shillings the average rent was eighteen shillings and sixpence. These did not represent the worst instances, neither were they isolated, the stories could be repeated in thousands of homes throughout the land. Back-to-back houses with narrow alleys between, where a dozen families shared a single communal tap like that depicted in the photograph of Long Bank,

Sunderland, were common in the north of England where over-crowding was endemic. The effect of bad housing and chronic overcrowding of the working class was accurately reflected in the disparity between the figures for infant mortality and disease for the lower paid against those of the better paid. Tuberculosis, rickets, scarlet fever and diphtheria proliferated among the poor, rotten housing combining with undernourishment to take a wicked toll of the health of working class children. In 1931, the Newport School Medical Officer found that boys at the age of fourteen at the High School were two inches taller and five pounds heavier than their contemporaries at the elementary school while the girls at the municipal secondary school were four inches higher and twenty-one pounds heavier than girls at the elementary schools. With slum housing came the tenants who paid no rent, the

bedbugs, fleas, cockroaches, mice and rats. The 'red army' to millions of the proletariat was not a revolutionary force but the battalions of fleas that infested their wretched homes. Bugs were burnt in candle flames as they crawled from behind peeling wall-paper and sulphur candles were burned in desperate efforts at fumigation. The nit comb ritual with mum combing the hair of her children onto a sheet of newspaper was a nightly practice. In the photograph sent from Swinton, two men are seen airing bedding after fumigation with arsenic before moving tenants from slum housing to new council houses. Fortunate were those whose names came up on the long waiting lists and they were even more fortunate if they had employment and could afford the rent when their turn arrived.

To many workers during the thirties, the 'divi' was as important as pay day and the declaration of the amount to be paid as dividend on purchases was awaited with desperate anticipation.

Dividend on purchases had been a wise element in the pioneers' scheme of co-operation for it had a strong appeal to the poor, of whom there were millions. It also accorded with their ideas on justice and equity that those members who had been the most loyal in shopping at the Co-operative should be better regarded than those who had been less loyal.

Despite the depression years the Co-ops flourished, having a close knowledge of the requirements of working class families and the prices they could afford to pay. The cash dividend would be paid out twice a year, varying from Society to Society but often paying two shillings in the pound. To a housewife who had traded steadily during the year, the money could bring an additional week's wages, arriving in time to buy new boots for the children or provide a few luxuries for Christmas.

Deep loyalty was bred during the inter-war years between workers and the Co-operatives, the movement frequently lending support to trade unions at times of distress. Free boot repairs for hunger marchers, free bread for strikers' children, extended credit in the form of food vouchers, interest free loans to unions during prolonged strikes and constant support for trade unionism through the Co-operative paper, *Reynolds News*, were not to be matched by the Home and Colonial Stores or *The Daily Mail*.

'Hopping' provided an annual working holiday for thousands of Londoners, who each summer escaped from the city to the hopfields of Kent. The hop season coincided with the slack time in the London docks and families from South and East London gladly volunteered year after year for the extra casual labour required at harvest time. At first light, sleepy children would be pulled from their beds, a wet flannel wiped across their faces, and still drooping with sleep be perched on barrows, laden with the necessities of life for the next three weeks. Pots, pans, candles, bedding, buckets, cutlery and clothing and children would be pushed to London Bridge Station for the journey to the countryside. On arrival in Kent, they would be met with horses and carts and driven to the farm and allocated a hut. Conditions were spartan but each family did its best to transform the bare huts into a comfortable home. Bundles of faggots would be provided to serve as fuel for the open air cooking fires as well as beds onto which mattresses stuffed with straw would be laid. All the family joined in the work of filling the bins with hops, picking five bushels for a shilling and no stray leaves to be included.

The highlight of the day, and of the holiday, would be the evenings, at the end of a hard day in the fields, with mum cooking a hot stew on the camp-fire and family and friends sitting around after dinner with mugs of hot cocoa, yarning by the flickering embers. The snapshot shows a typical related family group, the Monkfields, Yearleys and Jenkins from Bethnal Green and Hackney, in September 1928 at Chamber's Farm, Willington, Kent.

Sir Oswald Mosley came to the Labour Party via Winchester, Sandhurst, the Harrow Conservative Association and Cliveden, joining both the Labour Party and the Independent Labour Party in March 1924. Brilliant in debate, wealthy and well connected, he rose rapidly in the McDonald hierarchy and in the Labour government of 1929 was given the position of Chancellor of the Duchy of Lancaster, being appointed as one of the four ministers responsible for the problem of unemployment. His colleagues were J. H. Thomas, who had primary responsibility, George Lansbury and Tom Johnston. Mosley had a clear and practical policy for dealing with unemployment but was totally frustrated by Thomas who had little grasp of the intricacies of economics. Mosley saw Thomas as a 'drunken clown' and treated him with aristocratic contempt but could not persuade McDonald to sack the incompetent minister because of the strong trade union support he enjoyed and his influence in the Parliamentary Labour Party. Unable to implement his plans for dealing with unemployment, Mosley resigned in May 1931 and put his proposals directly to the House on 28 May. Despite an acclaimed speech, Mosley mustered only twenty-nine votes and left to publish his proposals as *The Mosley Manifesto*, signed by seventeen supporters including Bevan, A. J. Cook, W. J. Brown and John Strachey. Mosley then announced the forming of the New Party and was joined in the formation by four MPs and given substantial financial support by Lord Nuffield.

The turn to facism was swift. Mosley formed New Party Youth Clubs aimed at providing physical fitness and political training, their duties to include keeping order at public meetings—his storm troopers of tomorrow. Many of the prominent people who had supported the New Party recognised the signs of emerging fascism had departed, though Mosley was to enjoy considerable financial support from wealthy industrialists for years to come. By October 1932, the New Party mask was off and Mosley founded the British Union of Fascists complete with Nazi style regalia. His storm

troopers were his 'Blackshirts', the élite of them housed in barracks at Chelsea appropriately named the Black House, complete with parade ground. Mosley claimed that in an emergency the Black House could become a self-contained unit for five thousand of his troops. His Blackshirts wore a simple black uniform, the shirt made in fencing style in deference to their leader's prowess in that sport, while his officers aped their Nazi counterparts wearing tunic jackets, shiny peaked caps, breeches and the inevitable jack boots. Lord Rothermere was a staunch protagonist for Mosley and on 15 January 1934, his *Daily Mail* appeared with the headline, 'Hurrah for the Blackshirts'. Mosley held military style rallies, miniature Nuremburgs, at which he could posture as a British Führer and they were the scenes of mass opposition from the Communists and later, the United Front. In 1934, at the peak of the strength of the British fascists, estimated at forty thousand, organised in four hundred branches, Mosley led three big rallies, at the Albert Hall, Hyde Park and Olympia. At the Olympia rally the blackshirts, anxious to demonstrate their efficiency as storm troopers shocked the nation with the violence of their attacks upon protesters inside the hall. In 1936, when the anti-semetic outbursts of the fascists were reaching a climax. Mosley planned a provocative military march of his uniformed racists through the heart of Whitechapel. Mosley completely underestimated the depth of feeling against his creed of hate and more than two hundred thousand Londoners, Jews and Gentiles, rallied under the Spanish anti-facist slogan 'they shall not pass'. They did not and it proved a decisive blow from which the British fascists never fully recovered.

The photograph shows Mosley and two thousand of his fascists out of uniform (banned by the Public Order Act of 1936 following the Battle of Cable Street), ringed by a solid wall of clenched fists from twenty-five thousand United Front anti-fascists in July 1937.

The 'Big Meeting' has been an annual event in the mining life of the Durham coalfields for more than a century, a combination of a giant beano and solemn reaffirmation of faith in the solidarity of the union. The first of the gala events was held at Wharton Park in 1871 and set the pattern of pageant and politics, with miners walking from the colliery villages, carrying banners and drawing their sweethearts and wives in open decorated carts. They heard Alexander McDonald, the first of the miners MPs, denounce Brancepeth Colliery for working boys for fifteen and sixteen hours a day and joined heartily in singing a song written by a poetic miner from Staffordshire

> All men are equal in His sight
> The bond, the free, the black, the white
> He made them all, then freedom gave,
> He made the man, man made the slave.

Each year after, tens of thousands would pour into Durham City from early morning, carried from the surrounding pit villages by the steam trains of the North Eastern Railway Company. Shopkeepers boarded their windows against the invasion of the men with muscles of steel while public houses threw open their doors to help wash away the coal dust and sweeten the singing.

In 1875, the directors of the railway company withdrew the local trains to Durham on Gala Days, giving as their reason that they could not transport so many people on a Saturday. The miners accustomed to holding their meetings in the face of magistrates and military solved the problem by holding their next two annual Gala Days on Mondays!

The 'Big Meeting' grew to be a pageant of working class celebration and culture. Every lodge had a banner and most had a

band. It became a matter of pride to be one of the team to buckle on leather harness and hoist the massive silken sail of colour, the lodge banner, and march at the head of lodge and community to the rasping marches of silver or brass. For the mothers and wives it was a release from the routine of bathing men in front of the kitchen range at the end of the shift, the endless struggle to clean and dry heavy coal-black pit clothes, the scrimping to conjure meals bought on starvation wages. For the whole family it was a day of escape and for most, the only outing of the year.

The miners invited guest speakers by popular vote and the Gala became a barometer of popularity for Labour leaders. Over the years, the list reads as a roll-call of pioneers, from the anarchist Prince Kropotkin, Tom Mann, Keir Hardie, John Burns and Havelock Wilson in the nineteenth century, to Robert Smillie, A. J. Cook, Ellen Wilkinson, Aneurin Bevan, Mannie Shinwell and Michael Foot in the twentieth century.

In its greatest days, more than a hundred banners and bands would accompany the marchers, packing the streets with music and dancing as they proceeded to the Durham racecourse and a finale of roundabouts, lemonade, beer and speeches.

The photographs capture two aspects of the Durham Miners' Gala in the thirties. The men relaxed before the lodge banner, all in their Sunday best, the children eating, the young wives happy to have their families together. The other gives an impression of a community on holiday as they pour forth from a train at Chester-le-Street, the bandsmen in uniform, ready to take the City for a day. Tomorrow, back into the fearful blackness, their resolve strengthened by the vision of a better tomorrow, eloquently and impassionedly foretold by the speakers at the 'Big Meeting'.

Taken at Wigan in the 1930s this picture is reminiscent of the
photographs of pit-brow lasses taken at the end of the nineteenth
century. Surprisingly, well over three thousand women were still
employed at coal mines in 1930, working at sidings, tramways and
washing and sorting coal. Two hundred and thirty-nine were girls
under the age of sixteen and more than half (1,711) of the total
were employed in the Lancashire and Cheshire districts where the
tradition of women colliery workers was strongest. There were
sixteen mines in operation at Wigan when the photograph was
taken and it is believed that the scene is from the largest of these,
owned by the Wigan Coal Corporation Limited.

While millions lived in respect-destroying poverty, harassed by mean officials and living a humiliating life 'on the dole', other sections of British society were paradoxically enjoying a boom. Mass production was not confined to the emerging motor industry, and the fashion business in particular had adopted American methods in producing for the popular market. Though competition was fierce, with multiples such as Montague Burton and the Fifty Shilling Tailors challenging each other in the High Street, clothing was an expanding home market. The numbers employed in tailoring increased by one hundred percent between 1921 and 1938 to a record fifty thousand. The Tailor and Garment Workers' Union recruited heavily during the late thirties and despite anti-trade union opposition from some companies made substantial progress in the organisation of the major manufacturers.

The Ideal Clothiers, where this picture was taken at their Elsden Road factory in Wellingborough in 1937, was one of the big producers that accepted the complete unionisation of their staff. Employing more than two thousand workers at eight factories, engaged in the manufacture of men's, ladies' and children's tailored outerwear, all employees were members of the Tailors and Garment Workers' Union. Conditions of employment contrasted sharply with the familiar sweat shops of the tailoring trade and a progressive management offered the rare security of a non-contributory pension fund.

Spain was the catalyst that brought a greater degree of united action within the ranks of the organised labour movement than any other political issue of the thirties. Michael Foot has written that 'Spain cut the knot of emotional and intellectual contradictions in which the left had been entangled ever since Hitler came to power. Suddenly the claims of international law, class solidarity and the desire to win the Soviet Union as an ally fitted into the same strategy.' The passionate cry from Madrid in response to the fascist revolt 'it is better to die on your feet than live on your knees' reverberated throughout the labour left. While Bevin, Citrine and Dalton won the Trades Union Congress in September 1936 for the Eden-Baldwin policy of non-intervention, informal discussions were being held by Cripps, Pollitt and William Mellors on the possibility of united action in support of the Spanish Republic. Earlier that summer Victor Gollancz, Harold Laski and John Strachey had launched the spectacularly successful Left Book Club, preparing the ground for a Popular Front and in January 1937 the first issue of *Tribune* was published, the controlling board included Bevan, Cripps, Laski, Brailsford and Ellen Wilkinson.

On 24 January 1937, the United Campaign was launched at a great meeting at the Manchester Free Trade Hall, the platform being shared by Stafford Cripps, Jimmy Maxton, Harry Pollitt and William Mellors. Among the principal signatories to the manifesto were Nye Bevan, Tom Mann, William Gallacher, H. N. Brailsford, Frank Horrabin and Fenner Brockway. As the right wing fought back, the United Front packed meeting after meeting with thousands of Labour, Communist, ILP Socialist League and trade union supporters, organising practical aid for their Spanish comrades with devoted intensity. The picture of men and women

queuing with an anti-facist banner was taken at Belle Vue, Manchester, in 1938, and shows Margaret Whalley and Mary Eckersley both members of the New Cross Ward Labour Party waiting to attend one of the United Front rallies. Popular mass meetings such as these in all the main towns and cities helped to contain the right wing with their threats of bans and proscriptions. Eventually the Popular Front won wide acceptance, David Lloyd George appeared on the same platform as Harry Pollitt and Clement Attlee went to visit the International Brigade in Spain and gave the clenched fist salute.

May Day, 1938, was one of the largest since 1926 and the message was 'Spain above all'. Herbert Morrison, speaking from the Labour platform, said 'Let us remember the heroic Spanish people and their fight against foreign invasion for the freedom of the whole world.' Hammersmith Labour Party carried a banner announcing that it had collected five hundred pounds to send an ambulance to Spain and West London engineers paraded a motor cycle ambulance of the type they had sent. Everywhere in the procession were the tricolour flags of the Spanish Republic and a red banner, rippling in the breeze proclaimed 'Spain's fight is our fight'. Tens of thousands assembled at the eight platforms in Hyde Park to hear speakers from every section of the labour movement call for arms for Spain and the end of the Chamberlain government. As the long column of marchers entered the park, the loudest cheers came for wounded members of the International Brigade, closely followed by a group of women of the Spanish Medical Aid Committee, dressed in nurses' uniforms, collecting coins in a large white sheet to buy milk for Spanish children.

By the winter of 1938-39, the National Unemployed Workers' Movement had changed their tactics from national marches and demonstrations to a series of localised stunts aimed at focusing attention to their demands for winter relief. Their three point programme called for additional winter unemployment payments of two shillings and sixpence per adult and one shilling per child. They also demanded a national scheme of public works at trade union rates of pay and the opportunity to put their case direct to the ministers concerned.

On 20 December 1938 two hundred poorly clad unemployed men made their way to Oxford Street, crowded with Christmas shoppers. As the hands of a giant clock on a department store moved to 3.15 p.m. the men stepped from the pavements and laid down in the roadway bringing the heavy traffic to an abrupt halt. The weather was bitterly cold and snow had been falling as the men covered themselves with posters calling for bread, work and winter relief.

Two days later, a hundred men strolled into the Grill Room of the Ritz Hotel, seating themselves at the tables laid for dinner. This sensation was followed by the capture of UAB offices by the unemployed, the flying of a banner from the Monument in London and the unemployed chaining themselves to the railings of labour exchanges.

Overshadowing the problem of unemployment was the threat of war. In 1938, the government began the distribution of thirty eight million gas masks to the civilian population in readiness for the war to come. In an endeavour to persuade children to don the claustrophobic, rubber-smelling objects, an imaginative 'Mickey-Mouse' adaption of the adult mask was designed, using red rubber for the face and blue eye-rims and nosepiece.

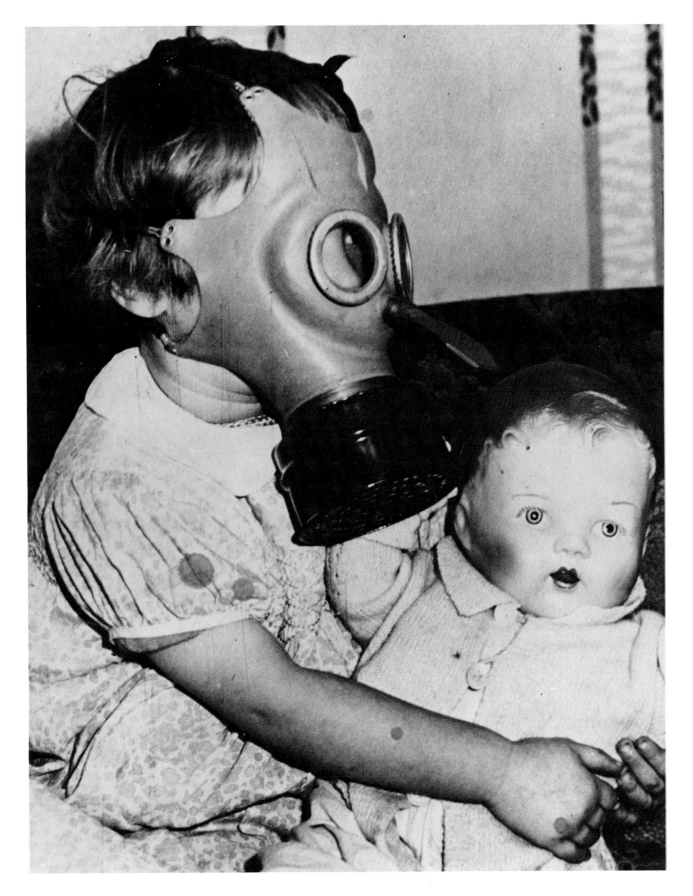

1940

The lesson of the fascist bombing of Guernica on 26 April 1937 was not entirely ignored by the Chamberlain government, despite their acquiescence. Cities were vulnerable to air bombardment and the civilian population would be a prime target in any Nazi attack. By September 1939, the British government had published plans for the evacuation of two million from London and the southern cities. As the threat of war grew in the summer of 1939, evacuation began and by 7 September, one year before the opening of the blitz on London, more than three and a half million people had been moved to safe areas. The social effects on all sections of the community were traumatic, though the greatest hardship fell upon the working class of whom more than a million were still unemployed at the outbreak of war.

Billeting arrangements were often chaotic. Pamela Hutchby, a ten year old girl, exhausted and travel-dirty after a slow train journey to Stafford recalls being driven from house to house, the billeting officer asking, 'do you want an evacuee?' 'What is it?' came the reply. 'A girl.' 'Sorry, we wouldn't mind a boy, but not a girl.' Even more shattering, the reply 'How much?' 'Ten and six a week!'

Sarah Blackshaw, a cockney mum with a baby, remembered standing on Ipswich station and being left unchosen from a line of evacuees as farmers took their pick as though selecting cattle, their first choice being strong lads who would be of most help on the farm. Elsewhere, middle class families recoiled as billeting officers attempted to place poorly dressed and underfed kids into their genteel homes, a world of oak biscuit barrels and fretwork-cased radiograms. Happily, there were those who took and treated the city refugees as their own children and formed deep relationships that survived the war.

The picture shows schoolchildren from Walthamstow, London, on their way to Blackhorse Road Station for evacuation.

As the British Expeditionary Force was driven back to the beaches of Dunkirk, Britain prepared for the seemingly inevitable invasion. On 30 May 1940, an order was made that 'no person shall display or cause or permit to be displayed any signs which furnish any indication of the name of, or the situation or direction of, or the distance to any place.' The idea was the creation of a geographically anonymous state to confuse the enemy should he land on this island. Road signs, street names, and station names were removed, if not to the confusion of the enemy who never arrived, but to the considerable confusion of the natives who awaited him.

The pictures of the labour intensive activity of railway workers at Esher removing the vitreous enamel sign for Esher and Sandown Park and replacing it back to front, are of a scene repeated throughout the railway stations of Britain. Destination boards were removed from buses and trams and underground station platform names were covered and replaced with letters three inches in height. Peering through the tiny areas of window not blacked out onto gloomy platforms, searching for recognition made journeying a nightmare for the inexperienced traveller. Milestones and post offices had their names obliterated and such was the totality and effectiveness of the loss of identity that the armed forces had to request a partial restoration of signs as they could not find their way about.

As the threat of invasion passed, the regulations were relaxed and the names gradually re-appeared during 1942 and 1943.

The civilian response to the government's broadcast appeal on 14 May 1940, for the formation of Local Defence Volunteer forces to help meet the threat of invasion, brought one and a half million volunteers within six weeks. An appeal for firearms was answered with twenty thousand shotguns and rifles being handed in and all sections of the community joined together in forming a virtually self-governing people's army. This did not altogether meet with the approval of War Office Blimps who had serious doubts about arming the working class outside military control and by August, the LDV was regularised as the Home Guard.

Despite the early inadequacies of arms and equipment and the passing aberration of a junior minister, Lord Croft, who issued pikes for street fighting, the Home Guard was to make a substantial contribution to the war effort by releasing the armed forces from many routine guard and patrol duties. The Home Guard grew to a strength of a million and three-quarters organised in eleven hundred battalions, many of these based at large factories, railway companies, docks and transport depots. In 1940, they waited for an invasion that never came, the only encounter with the enemy being the capture of the occasional baled-out German airman. In this role, the 3rd Renfrewshire Battalion Home Guard did have the distinction of taking prisoner the Deputy Führer of the Third Reich, Rudolph Hess, when he landed his Messerschmitt in Scotland in search of the Duke of Hamilton in 1941.

Perhaps the spirit of the Home Guard is captured by the inscription on the memorial mounted to the Number One Company, Falmouth HG, on the coastal path from Falmouth to the Mawnan Smith Parish Boundary. Headed 'For Freedom' it reads. . .'who during 1940, 41, 42, 43, 44, after their day's work, nightly patrolled this coast, armed and vigilant against German landings. Thus they watched 1,000 dawns appear across these great waters which form our country's moat.'

Ernest Bevin, Minister of Labour and National Service, is seen inspecting the 101 London Battalion, Home Guard.

At 3.50 p.m. on 7 September 1940, the Nazis began their blitz on London, the target being the London docks, the solid working class areas of Canning Town, Silvertown, Poplar, Bermondsey and Deptford bearing the full force of the first onslaught. In the little terraced houses that had back gardens, the people took to their Anderson shelters, dug into the earth, but for tens of thousands in tenements and houses without gardens there were no deep shelters, only inadequate brick-built surface shelters. Buildings with large cellars opened them to the public and conditions were often appalling as thousands crammed into them night after night.

People looked enviously at the London Underground stations, deep, warm and well lit, but official policy was against the use of them as shelters. Some overcame officialdom by buying platform tickets and staying put. In Stepney, the strong local Communist Party broke down gates when the stations closed and led people down to the platforms. Faced with the dreadful conditions in makeshift public shelters like those at Tilbury Arches and Mickey's Cellar in Stepney, together with rising protests from representative bodies like the West Ham Trades Council, the authorities relented and opened the underground stations as night shelters. At first, people simply took a few blankets and slept on the platforms like those in the photograph taken at Piccadilly in October 1940. Others slept on the lines after the current was switched off and even on the escalators. Seventy-nine stations were used as deep shelters and at the peak 177,000 people were sleeping in them each night. It was not until after the blitz in 1941 that bunks were installed.

By June 1941 two million homes had been damaged or destroyed by German bombing, over sixty percent of the destruction having been inflicted upon London. While the main onslaught was directed at the capital, other cities and ports were subjected to severe attacks over short concentrated periods or single raids. The ten hour incendiary and explosive blitz upon Coventry caused tremendous damage, literally overnight.

The problem of dealing with the homeless as a result of the raids was enormous and chaos often prevailed as rest centres and town halls were swamped with the brave but shaken survivors. The photograph taken at Plymouth after the two nights of blitz on 20 and 21 March 1941, reminds the viewer of the personal distress and organisational problems that remained after the 'all clear' sounded. After the injured had been treated, the missing searched for and the dead buried, furniture had to be removed and stored, damaged buildings demolished or patched up and accommodation found for the 'bombed out'. The raids on Plymouth alone left thirty thousand homeless and many fled the city centre together with some fifty thousand of the population that sought safety in the surrounding countryside, sleeping in barns, churches, quarry tunnels and even ditches.

The poverty of the working class was startingly revealed to many middle class voluntary workers when disinfecting and storing the few sticks of furniture that represented a family's home. One London writer commented that most of the furniture was so poor and worn that it was a pity that it had not been completely destroyed.

The most spectacular and popular public meetings of the war were undoubtedly those calling for the opening of a second front in Europe. The belief that if Russia went down before the Nazi invaders, all would be lost for Britain, gripped the bomb battered civilian imagination and turned to hero worship as the Red Army repulsed the fascist forces at the threshold of Moscow. Though the Communist Party led the campaign for the second front, support was by no means confined to the left. As early as July 1941, *The Evening Standard* leader had said 'our business is now to create the second front.' At a meeting at the Stoll Theatre in December 1941, Aneurin Bevan shared the platform with Harry Pollitt in calling for the opening of a second front, the meeting being so well supported that the speeches had to be relayed to nine other full halls.

Popular support for the second front movement was encouraged by a deep rooted distrust that working people held for generals and politicians who before the Nazi invasion of Russia had been fanatically anti-Soviet. It was a widely held view that it was the considered policy of such people to leave the Russians and Germans to fight each other to destruction. As the Red Army won a series of victories, so the clamour for a second front increased, the logic of forcing Hitler to divide his forces winning increasing support from the Americans. In March 1942, President Roosevelt wrote to Churchill, 'your people and mine demand the establishment of a front to draw off the pressure on the Russians.' In April, Lord Beaverbrook made an outspoken speech in the United States in support of the second front, while at home, the massive rallies of support continued until the invasion finally took place in 1944.

The picture shows some of the sixty thousand people, mainly war workers, who gathered for a second front meeting at Trafalgar Square in July 1942.

The location and date of this photograph is unknown, although the period is clearly from the Second World War and it derives from the office of the National Union of Tailors and Garment Workers in Glasgow.

It would seem to be a union organised dance for servicemen, possibly for serving members of the NUTGW. The women's wartime fashions of wide shoulders, puffed sleeves, bare legs or black market stockings and flat-heeled shoes help us to speculate as to the tunes to which they danced. If taken in the later years of the war, say about 1943-4, it is a reasonable assumption that 'Shine On Victory Moon', was played, as well as old favourites like the Vera Lynn hit, 'The White Cliffs of Dover' and the Anglo-German forces choice, 'Lily Marlene', first recorded in Britain by Anne Shelton.

The music would have been live, dancing to a radiogram unusual and the concept of 'discos' unknown. No doubt there was a last waltz and the photograph lingers as a charming period picture that demonstrates the value of photographing the ordinary.

The fall of France in 1940 meant the loss of Britain's most important overseas coal market and caused a consequent rise in unemployment, particularly among the miners of South Wales. With a shortage of labour in the war industries, it hardly needed the exhortation of Ernest Bevin, Minister of Labour, to persuade the miners to seek work that was safer, cleaner and better paid in the munitions factories. Warnings by mining MPs that the dispersal of labour would lead to a crisis in coal production went unheeded, and by 1943 there were not enough men and boys available to produce the tonnage required to sustain the war effort. Men called up for the armed services were given the option of going to the pits but a mere three thousand preferred the coalfields to the battlefields. Bevin told the Miners' Federation conference in July 1943 that 'desperate remedies' would have to be taken to meet the need of more manpower. The remedy chosen by Bevin was compulsory conscription for mining among the youths of Britain. A ballot system was introduced among the eighteen year olds as they registered for military service and those with a balloted digit as the final numeral of their registration number were packed off for pit training and then into the battle for coal.

The lads were billeted out in the mining areas and given a lodging allowance of twenty-five shillings a week. Despite the friendly welcome given to them by the colliers, there was a deep resentment and discontent among the youths who had been arbitrarily chosen for the pits. There were complaints about the inadequacy of the pay which did not allow enough for lodging, fares, laundry and pit clothes and 'Bevin boys' walked out from the Askern colliery, Doncaster, and strikes were threatened from Newcastle to Kent. As a result, the wages were increased on 25 January 1944 from two pounds ten shillings and sixpence to three pounds per week. The picture of Bevin boys leaving St. Pancras Station for Chesterfield in January 1944 to commence their training clearly expresses their lack of enthusiasm for life as a miner.

Whatever it meant to the politicians, to the rank and file soldiers, British, Russian and American, the link up of allied forces from the west with Russian troops from the east, meant that the war would soon be over.

The first contact was made by the River Elbe, at Torgau on 28 April 1945, when troops of the US 1st Army commanded by General Courtney Hodges, joined with Soviet troops of the 1st Ukranian Army led by Marshall Koniev. Lieutenant William D. Robertson recounted how the two armies shared wine, sardines and chocolate in an impromptu celebration of the historic meeting. President Truman sent a telegram to Stalin saying '. . . . . the Anglo-American armies under the command of General Eisenhower have met the Soviet forces where they intended to meet, in the heart of Nazi Germany. The enemy has been cut in two.'

British troops met the Soviets as Rokossovsky's army entered Mecklenburg. The photograph shows a British lance corporal greeting a young Russian tankman. The Soviet armies had come a long way, from the Volga, over the Dneiper, Vistula, Oder and Spree and the British who had been driven from Europe at Dunkirk, rejoiced in joining hands with their allies in the final destruction of fascism.

On the day that the Western allies met up with the Russians, Mussolini was hanged head downwards by Italian partisans in a petrol station in Milan. On 4 May the German army in the west surrendered to General Montgomery at Lüneburg Heath.

The news of the unconditional surrender of Germany began to trickle through on 7 May and the following day was officially celebrated as VE Day (Victory in Europe) by a jubilant outburst of public celebration, official and unofficial.

In the working class districts of the bomb damaged cities bonfires were simply built in the middle of the roadways and kept burning throughout the night and for much of the next day. There was no shortage of fuel for the timber from bombed houses was never far from the joyous crowds that danced, cried, sang and rejoiced at their deliverance from war and fascism. In West Ham, the worst bombed borough in London, more than £8,000 worth of damage was caused to the roads by victory fires and the enthusiasm of the people was not restricted to burning bomb damaged timber. In one street, a chimney-sweep's barrow standing outside his house was shamelessly wheeled onto the fire and youths had to be restrained from lifting the gates to the churchyard from their hinges to add to the conflagration.

The streets were festooned with flags of the allies, bunting and painted V signs, that were to remain to welcome home absent husbands, fathers, sons and daughters from the armed services.

In one street in Stratford, East London, bricklayers repairing the bomb damaged wall of a house, built into the wall two brick V signs to remain as a memorial to the momentous victory and the uninhibited celebrations that followed.

The photograph was taken at Havering Street, Stepney, East London.

'The victory of free men and women over Nazism and Facism is a challenge to us all. . . . .shall we face again poverty and unemployment. . . . .we have brought freedom to so many people. Let us now liberate ourselves.' These excerpts from the1945 election address of Sidney Silverman gave voice to the popular demand to be rid of Tory power. At the Labour Party Conference before the General Election, Bevan whipped up the emotional fervour, 'our aim', he said 'was the political extinction of the Tory Party.'

Churchill tried desperately to bluff the electorate in the tradition of Conservative electioneering, reminiscent of the Zinoviev forgery in 1931 and the Post Office Savings scare of 1935, by broadcasting on 4 June 1945, 'I declare to you that no Socialist system can be established without a political police. They would have to fall back on some sort of Gestapo.' The answer of the people came on 26 July, the majority voting for democratic socialism and the programme of the Labour Party, outlined in the election manifesto *Let us face the future.*

Just forty-five years after the meeting in the Memorial Hall, Farringdon Road, set the alliance of trade unionists and socialists on the journey to Parliamentary power, 393 Labour members were elected to implement the building of a socialist Britain. For millions, this was the millennium. Never before had a government been elected with such enthusiasm and with such a mandate for radical social change. Bonfires were lit in the streets, old men openly wept with joy, for the long, long night was over. In the House of Commons the party stood and sang The Red Flag to the disbelief and demoralised bewilderment of the Conservative opposition.

Clement Attlee had awaited the election result at Transport House and calmly accepted the victory. With him, second on the left, front row in the photograph was Arthur Deakin, acting General Secretary of the Transport and General Workers' Union.

A week after VE Day, Ernest Bevin, Minister of Labour in the wartime coalition government announced that demobilisation of the armed forces would begin on 18 June, priority being given to building workers and those who could be engaged on reconstruction. Threequarters of a million were to be home by the end of the year and the rest would follow in orderly fashion until over four million had returned to civilian life. Just where some of them were return to, was another problem. By the end of the war, Britain had suffered damage or destruction of four million homes as a result of Nazi air attacks. Britain had a housing shortage and millions of slum houses before the war began. Six years of neglect and enemy bombardment combined with a world shortage of building materials to create the worst housing crisis in its history. For too many the victorious return home was to derelict tenements, damp basements or delapidated terraced housing awaiting war damage repair. For the even less fortunate, there was no family home to return to at all and homecoming meant the rest centre or crowded and embarrassing shared occupancy with relatives or friends.

'Welcome hame lads' was scrawled on the walls of Glasgow tenements and though the greeting from loved ones was undoubtedly warm, the prospect was surely bleak. To aggravate the situation and add to the sense of frustration felt by the homeless and inadequately housed, large numbers of government requisitioned buildings stood empty and in the rich suburbs of the cities there was no shortage of houses for those with three or four thousand pounds to spend, though the gratuity for a time-served ex-serviceman was likely to be nearer fifty pounds.

In 1946, the Communist Party launched a campaign to move homeless families into empty camps, vacant mansions and hotels. Squatters, as they became known, moved into the one hundred room Castle Roy in Dundee, the Ivanhoe Hotel in London and occupied what had been the largest US camp in Britain: Dawes Hill at High Wycombe. Homeless families moved their furniture into Duchess of Bedford House, Kensington (seen in photograph), on 11 September 1946, and defied the attempts of the Ministry of Works officials to eject them.

Official reaction was mixed. In some areas councils allowed the connection of essential services to occupied buildings while others did just the opposite. Reading Council threatened to remove squatters from the housing list and others instructed the Food Office to refuse registration for milk. Trade unionists frequently gave support, building workers refusing to dismantle huts at the Hyde Park gun site and electricians sent to a block of luxury flats

in West London declining to cut off the supply of power. At Burnham, Buckinghamshire, Canadian soldiers helped squatters to carry in their furniture to the camp as the army pulled out. Eventually, five Communist leaders were charged with conspiracy and, ably defended by Sir Walter Monkton, KC, were bound over for two years. The Communists may have relented in their political campaign but the problems remained and others sought the same solution to homelessness. In 1948, a member of the National Union of Agricultural Workers, Mr F. C. Grainger, a gardener, was arbitrarily dismissed from his job and given notice to quit the cottage that was tied to the job. Grainger, with his wife and seven children, moved into empty property at Northallerton known as the Old Police Houses. When the Council decided to renovate the property they obtained an eviction order and once again the family were homeless. When prisoners of war moved out of the Stone Cross Hostel at Northallerton, the Graingers moved in and the picture shows Mrs Grainger with six of her children getting tea ready in one of the former POW hostel huts (on previous page).

The Labour government was quick to honour its pledge to nationalise the mines, the terms of the Coal Industry Nationalisation Bill being published on 21 December 1945. Eventually, after passage through the Commons and the formation of the Coal Board, the vesting date was set on 1 January 1947.

Whatever the misgivings held by many trade unionists on the final structure of the administration of the industry, the miners, after generations of abject poverty, exploitation and fierce struggle, acclaimed with enthusiasm the Act that passed the ownership of the mines to the people. For the 1947 Durham Gala, the miners invited Ernest Bevin, Herbert Morrison, Michael Foot and Arthur Horner as their guest speakers, already having welcomed Attlee, Bevan and Dalton the previous year. These were the heroes of the hour and the portraits of the Labour leaders were emblazoned in recognition on the silken banners of the lodges. Cripps and Bevin appeared on the Middridge Drift Lodge banner, Bevan on Murton and Craghead, Dalton on Randolph and Attlee on a number, including the East Hetton Lodge seen in the photograph taken outside the Royal County Hotel, Durham. The colliers and their families danced in the streets as they celebrated the momentous event of this, the seventy-sixth Gala. The pictorial illustrations and slogans that were to adorn the lodge banners throughout the mining communities of Britain left no doubt as to

the importance the miners gave to nationalisation.
Risca, South Wales, hailed 'Nationalisation, the dawn of a new
era'. Dysart, Scotland, summed up past and present, 'Anticipation
1888, Desperation 1921-26, Realisation 1943, Nationalisation
1947'. Shinwell, the Minister of Fuel and Power, was painted
handing the deed of nationalisation to Lord Hyndley, first
chairman of the National Coal Board. Yorkshire miners at
Wombwell illustrated their banner with a miner climbing the steps
of labour achievement, nationalisation, five day week, social
security, family allowances, health and peace, leading to the final
goal of socialism. It was a euphoria born of generations of
oppression; for the old miners, this was the millennium, for the
young, their hope for the future. Hamsterely Lodge epitomised
this by painting their banner with a scene of an old miner at the
pithead, pointing to the revitalised colliery and saying to a young
miner, 'now it's up to you.'
The photograph of George Short, who was born in 1872 and
started work underground at the age of twelve, perfectly enshrines
the mood of 1947. In his face, a life of work and hardship, proudly
alongside the banner of the NCB, the mines for the people, hope
realised at the end of a working life, a dignified conclusion and a
better beginning.

The London Trades Council had actively participated in every official trade union May Day demonstration in the capital since the first international labour day in 1890. Throughout the decades the annual pageant of working class power had been celebrated by trade unionists marching through the streets, bands playing, banners flying in earnest though festive parades of strength and intent. In 1949, the LTC booked Trafalgar Square for a rally on 1 May and prepared to organise the march. That year the freedom of trade unionists to parade the streets was astonishingly curtailed. Sir Oswald Mosely, leader of the pre-war British Union of Fascists, had re-emerged into political life forming the new Union Movement in February 1948. For some time his former henchmen, notably Jeffrey Hamm, had been holding regular open air meetings in the East End market at Ridley Road, Dalston, where many of the stallholders were Jewish. Nor surprisingly, the meetings were the scene of violent opposition as the old fascists appeared under their new name. When Mosely announced his intention to march from Ridley Road through Stamford Hill to Tottenham, thousands of ex-servicemen, Jew and Gentile, gathered in Kingsland High Road to prevent the provocation. East London mayors called upon the Home Secretary to ban the fascist marches and on 22 March 1949, Chuter Ede announced a ban on all political processions. Assurance was sought that trade union marches did not fall within the compass of the ban, but on 31 March, the Home Secretary said in the Commons that the forthcoming LTC march was included in the ban.

For the first time since 1890, London trade unionists were deprived of their freedom to march on May Day, the ban being imposed by a Labour Home Secretary in the strongest Labour government in British history.

The photograph shows a section of the vast crowd that gathered in the Square. Despite the ban, the London Trades Council held its usual rally in Trafalgar Square, thousands defying the Home Secretary and marching in with banners flying.

In 1949, clothes, boots and shoes were taken off ration and followed the lifting of restrictions the previous year on bread, potatoes and preserves. Remaining on ration were milk, tea, sugar, meat, bacon, butter, fats and soap, the fresh meat allocation being a microscopic eight pennyworth a week. Austerity was a word reiterated remorselessly by the anti-government press and bombed sites and derelict buildings remained as dusty and ugly reminders that post-war reconstruction was still at a beginning.

Labour, faced with the aftermath of six years of war had embarked on an ambitious programme of social reform, raising the school leaving age to fifteen, abolishing fees in state schools, nationalising the Bank of England, the railway companies, coal mines, electricity, gas, road haulage, airlines and cable and wireless companies. Comprehensive social security was introduced, family allowances, compensation for injury at work and the National Health Service was created despite considerable opposition.

If life was austere, it was better for the majority than it had been in the years before the war and Britain's industry was expanding. The photograph, of car workers on the assembly line at Cowley in 1946, gives a backward glance at the boom in production that was already underway by 1950. In 1945, only 16,938 cars were manufactured in Britain; by 1950 the figure had reached a record 522,515.

Attlee set the date of the general election as 23 February 1950, and the Labour Party fought the election on the manifesto *Let us win through together*, an endorsement of Cripps' economic policy. Despite polling a record 13.2 million votes, the Labour majority was cut to six and the future set for the development of consumer capitalism.

Source Notes to the Photographs

p.31 **Limeburners/Greenwich** Julian Watson, Local History Librarian, Greenich

p.32 **Carpenters/Carnoustie** T. J. Connelly, *The Woodworkers*, ASW London   S. Higenbottom, *Our Society's History*, ASW Manchester

p.33 **Eviction/Cherhill** *the English Labourer*, 26 February 1876

p.34 **Railwaymen/LB & SCR**

p. 35 **Railwaymen/Fence Houses** Philip S. Bagwell, *The Railwaymen*, George Allen & Unwin, London   Norman McKillop, *The Lighted Flame*, Thomas Nelson & Sons, London   G. W. Alcock, *Fifty Years of Railway Trade Unionism*, NUR London

p.36 **Coal trimmers** Fenner Brockway, *Hungry England*, Victor Gollancz, London   TUC Annual Report, 1895

p.37 **Factory explosion/Cornbrook** *Manchester Weekly Times and Examiner*, 25 June 1887   *Manchester Guardian*, 25 June 1887

p.38 **Aqueduct builders/Thirlmere** D. W. Barrett, *Life and Work Among the Navvies*, Society for Promotion of Christian Knowledge   D. Taylor, Central Library, Manchester

p.39 **Manchester Ship Canal** Sir Bosdin Leech, *History of the Manchester Ship Canal*, volume 2

p.40 **Pit brow lasses/1890** Angela V. John, *History Bulletin No. 3*, North West Group for the Study of Labour History   Account by Mrs H. M. Trett, great grandaughter of Thomas Burns

p.41 **Opening of Woolwich Free Ferry** *Woolwich Gazette*, 23 March 1889

p.42 **Dock Strike/Street feeding**

p.43 **End of Dock Strike** Ben Tillett, *Memories and Reflections*, John Long, London   John Lovell, *Stevedores and Dockers*, Macmillan, London   Ann Stafford, *A Match to Fire the Thames*, Hodder and Stroughton, London

p.45 **Harvester** Reg Groves, *Sharpen the Sickle*, The Porcupine Press, London   Pamela Horn, *Joseph Arch*, The Roundwood Press, Kineton   F. E. Green, *The Tyranny of the Countryside*, T. Fisher Unwin, London   R. C. Russell, *The Revolt of the Field in Lincs.*, Lincoln County Committee, NUAW

p.46 *Royal Oak* **Keel-laying** *Birkenhead & Cheshire Advertiser & Wallasey Guardian*, 31 May 1890

p.47 **Coopers/Sussex** Bob Gilding, *The Journeyman Coopers of East London*, History Workshop pamphlet No. 4, Ruskin College, Oxford

p.48 **Cavalry at Wentworth**

p.49 **Pleasley Colliery** J. J. Terrett, *The Right Hon. H. H. Asquith MP and the Featherstone Massacre*, Twentieth Century Press, London   R. Page Arnot, *The Miners*, George Allen & Unwin, London   J. E. Williams, *The Derbyshire Miners*, George Allen & Unwin, London   Alan R. Griffin, *The Nottinghamshire Miners*, Nottingham area, NUM   *Justice*, 15 July and 16 September 1893   *Mansfield Reporter*, 13 October 1893   Judith A Schofield, Librarian Brian O'Malley Central Library and Arts Centre, Rotherham

p.50 **Mersey carters** *Liverpool Review*, 1 March 1890

p.51 **Miners/Ty Tryst** Ness Edwards, *History of the South Wales Miners' Federation*, Lawrence & Wishart, London   R. Page Arnot, *The Miners*, George Allen & Unwin, London   *Pontypridd Observer*, June 1898   *Rhondda Post*, June 1898   *Pontypridd Chronicle*, June 1898

p.52 **Ragged School** J. Wesley Bready, *Lord Shaftesbury and Social Industrial Progress*, George Allen & Unwin, London   J. L. & B. Hammond, *Lord Shaftesbury*, Constable, London   F. Smith, *A History of English Elementary Education, 1760-1902*, University of London Press   Gareth Stedman Jones, *Outcast London*, Clarendon Press, Oxford

p.53 **Cotton spinners** H. A. Turner, *Trade Union Growth, Structure & Policy, Comparative Growth of the Cotton Unions*, George Allen & Unwin, London   R. G. Kirkby and A. E. Musson, *Voice of the People*, Manchester University Press   John Jewkes and E. M. Gray, *Wages & Labour in the Lancashire Cotton Spinning Industry*, Manchester University Press

p.54 **Farthing breakfast queue**

p.55 **Farthing breakfasts** Robert H. Shepherd, *Child Slaves of Britain*, Hurst and Blackett, London   Personal recollections of Lieutenant Colonel Cyril J. Barnes

p.57 **Mafeking celebration/Enfield** *Enfield & Edmonton Chronicle*, 17, 18, 25 May, 1900   Thomas Pakenham, *The Boer War*, Weidenfeld & Nicolson, London

p.58 **Living-in demonstration** P. C. Hoffman, *They Also Serve*, The Porcupine Press, London

p.59 **Destitute women/Embankment** Rodney Mace, *Trafalgar Square*, Lawrence & Wishart, London   General Booth, *In Darkest England and the Way Out*, Salvation Army, London   Gareth Stedman Jones, *Outcast London*, Clarendon Press, Oxford

p.60 **Coffin beds** George R. Sims, *Living London*, Cassell & Co. London

p.61 **Wash & brush up** George R. Sims, *Living London*, Cassell & Co. London

p.62 **Barefoot children/Playground**

p.63 **Barefoot children/Pie Shop**

p.64 **Slum children**

p.65 **Children with pushchair** Robert H. Sherrard, *Child Slaves of Britain*, Hurst & Blackett, London   Gareth Stedman Jones, *Outcast London*, Clarendon Press, Oxford   George R. Sims, *Living London*, Cassell & Co. London

p.66 **Boys chopping firewood** *Manchester & Salford Methodist Mission, 75th Anniversary Booklet*. M & SMM Manchester   M & SMM Annual Reports 1891-1910   Revd John Banks, MA

p.67 **Cleaning the flags** Harry Pollitt, *Serving My Time*, Lawrence & Wishart, London   Personal recollections of the author

p.68 **Carrow School**

p.69 **Men leaving work** Miss Helen C. Colman, *Carrow Works Magazine* volume 15 No. 3. July 1932   *Carrow Old School Boys' Association, Souvenir Brochure*, 19 May 1950

p.70 **Women brickmakers**

p.71 **Chainmakers** *Britain At Work*, Cassell & Co, London   Sheila Lewenhak, *Women and Trade Unions*, Ernest Benn Ltd., London

p.72 **Metal shearing machine** Chris Makepeace, *Manchester As It Was*, volume 3   Kenneth Hirst   Andrew Perry

p.73 **Tramway construction** *The Cornubian & Redruth Times*, 11 April 1902   L. F. Barham

p.74 **Raunds march**

p.75 **Raunds march** Alan Fox, *A History of the National Union of Boot and Shoe Operatives, 1874-1957*, Basil Blackwell, Oxford   *50th. Anniversary of Raunds March to London*, NUBSO, Northampton

p.76 **Leicester unemployed march**

p.77 **Men washing** *Leicester Daily Post*, 20 May-12 June 1905   *Hampstead & Highgate Gazette*, 10 and 17 June 1905

p.78 **Knocking up and mill girls** John Ackworth, *Clog Shop Chronicles*, Charles H. Kelly, London

p.79 **Westminster unemployed** H. W. Lee and E. Archbold, *Social Democracy in Britain*, Social Democratic Federation, London   *Justice*, November 1905

p.80 **Ernest Marklew** H. W. Lee and E. Archbold, *Social Democracy in Britain*, Social Democratic Federation, London   *The Nelson Leader*, 25 May-14 September 1906

p.81 **Manchester Cathedral/Unemployed** *Manchester Guardian*, 14 September 1908

p.82 **Caslon Letter Foundry** T. B. Read, *A History of Old English Letter Foundries*, Faber, London   *British Printer*, Vol. 18, December 1905 and January 1906. Vol. 23, June and July 1910

p.83 **Haggerston by-election** Simon Knott, *The Electoral Crucible*, (The politics of London 1900-1914) Greene & Co. London   Sylvia Pankhurst, *The Suffragette Movement*, Longmans, London   H. W. Lee and E. Archbold, *Social Democracy in Britain*, Social Democratic Federation, London   *Shoreditch Mail and North London Advertiser*, 31 July 1908   *Shoreditch Observer*, 31 July 1908   *Clarion*, 31 July and 1 August 1908   *Justice*, 25 July and 1 August 1908

p.84 **Ned Page**

p.85 **Stanley pit disaster funeral** Helen & Baron Duckham, *Great Pit Disasters*, David & Charles, Newton Abbot   *Durham Chronicle*, 19, 20 and 26 February 1909 and 15 March 1909   *The Times*, 18 and 20 February 1909 and 15 May 1909

p.87 **Durham mining family** W. A. Moyes, *Mostly Mining*, Frank Graham, Newcastle upon Tyne   R. Page Arnot, *The Miners*, George Allen & Unwin, London

p.88 **Radcliffe Co-op** G. Knights and A. Farrington, *History of the Radcliffe & Pilkington District Industrial Co-operative Society, 1860-1910*, Manchester Co-operative Newspaper society

p.89 **Lord Mayor's 'Good Bye'** *Manchester Guardian*, 15 April 1910   Letter to *Manchester Guardian* from Catherine Garett 3 May 1910

p.90 **Tom Mann**

p.91 **Soldiers and striker** *Marxism Today*, E. Frow & H. Hikins, March 1964   Henry Pelling, *A History of British Trade Unionism*, Penguin Books, London   Tom Mann, *Tom Mann's Memoirs*, The Labour Publishing Co. Ltd. London

p.92 **Troops at Clapham Junction** Philip Bagwell, *The Railwaymen*, George Allen & Unwin, London

p.93 **Bermondsey women's strike** Mary Agnes Hamilton, *Mary MacArthur*, Leonard Parsons, London   *Women's Trade Union League, Annual Report, 1911*   *Daily Chronicle*, 15 August 1911   *The Times*, 15 August 1911   *The Bermondsey & Southwark Gazette*, 17 August 1911

p.94 **Robertson's strike**

p.95 **Women drinking** *Shields Daily Gazette and Shipping Telegraph*, 14 June to 4 August 1914   Personal recollections of Joseph Walker, Edward Main, Wilhelmena Nightingale, James Robertson

p.96 **Street scene** Caption on back of photograph

p.97 **Clarion van** Jill Liddington and Jill Norris, *One Hand Tied Behind Us*, Virago, London   *Clarion*, 20 February, 15 March, 20 March, 3 April, 10 April and 1 May 1914

p.98 **Boots' builders' strike** R. W. Postgate, *The Builders' History*, Labour Publishing Co. London   *Daily Herald*, June 1914

p.99 **Sergeant and recruits** William Stewart, *J. Keir Hardie*, Independent Labour Party, London   R. A. and G. H. Radice, *Will Thorne*, George Allen & Unwin, London
p.100 **Women engineers**
p.101 **Women gas workers** William Gallacher, *Revolt on the Clyde*, Lawrence & Wishart, London   Sheila Lewenhak, *Women and Trade Unions*, Ernest Benn Ltd., London   Henry Pelling, *History of British Trade Unionism*, Penguin Books, London
p.102 **Horseflesh shop** E. M. H. Lloyd, *Experiments in State Control*, Oxford University Press   Sir William Beveridge, *British Food Control*, Humphrey Milford, Oxford   Robert Smillie, *My Life For Labour*, Mills & Boon, London
p.103 **Wounded soldiers** *The Statistics of the Military Effort of the British Empire, 1914-1920.* War Office, H.M.S.O. London
p.104 **Pig killing** Personal recollection of Alice Pattinson
p.105 **Leek show/Castleside** B. Williamson, 'The Leek', *Mining and Social Change*, ed. M. Bulmer, Croom Helm
p.106 **Domestic servants**
p.107 **Domestic training** Personal recollection of Alice Pattinson
p.108 **Eviction** F. E. Green, *The Tyranny of the Countryside*, T. Fisher Unwin, London   Philip Bagwell, *The Railwaymen*, George Allen & Unwin, London   Richard Fynes, *The Miners of Northumberland and Durham*, John Robinson Junior, Newcastle upon Tyne
p.109 **Poppy day demonstration** John Montgomery, *The Twenties*, George Allen & Unwin, London
p.111 **Park and Dare funeral** *The Rhondda Leader*, 15 July 1920   Account given by G. L. Clark, miner from Powys
p.112 **Ashington miners** J. Davison, *Northumberland Miners' History, 1919-1939*, Northumberland area, N.U.M. Newcastle upon Tyne
p.113 **Dockers' breakfast/Bevin** Alan Bullock, *The Life and Times of Ernest Bevin, Vol. 1.* Heinemann, London   Trevor Evans, *Bevin*, George Allen & Unwin, London
p.114 **Bread distribution/Poplar**
p.115 **Bodyguard/Poplar** Raymond Postgate, *George Lansbury*, Longmans, Green & Co. London   Charles W. Key, *Red Poplar*, Labour Publishing Co. London
p.116 **TUC charabanc** TUC Annual Report, 1923
p.117 **North Kensington Labour Party charabanc** Recollection of Joan Davis
p.118 **Drying clothes**
p.119 **Miner bathing** Gerard Noel, *The Great Lock-out of 1926*, Constable, London   Personal recollection of Alice Pattinson
p.120 **Boy in mine** R. Page Arnot, *The General Strike*, Labour Research Dept., London   Gerard Noel, *The Great Lock-out of 1926*, Constable, London   Raymond Postgate, *A Workers' History of the Great Strike*, The Plebs League, London   A. J. Cook, *The Nine Days*, Co-operative Printing Society, London
p.121 **The agitator** R. Page Arnot, *The General Strike*, Labour Research Dept., London   Gerard Noel, *The Great Lock-out of 1926*, Constable, London
p.122 **Builders' demonstration** Gerard Noel, *The Great Lock-out of 1926*, Constable, London
p.123|**Methil miners** Emile Burns, *General Strike*, Lawrence & Wishart, London
p.124 **Soup kitchen/Rotheram**
p.125 **Children in shop** Gerard Noel, *The Great Lock-out of 1926*, Constable, London   Personal recollection of Ellis Hibbert
p.126 **Ammunition unloaded** Caption on back of photograph
p.127 **Special police** George Glasgow, *General Strikes and Road Transport*, Geoffrey Bles, London   Margaret Morris, *The General Strike*, Penguin Books, London   Andy Durr, *Who Were the Guilty?*, Brighton Labour History Press   Ernie Trory, *Brighton and the General Strike*, Crabtree Press, Brighton   Personal recollection of Sgt. J. Gorman, 3rd Medium Artillery
p.128 *Flying Scotsman* **derailed** Personal recollection of William Muckle, (sentenced to imprisonment for his part in the episode).
p.129 **End of strike** Philip Bagwell, *The Railwaymen*, George Allen & Unwin, London   Julian Symons, *The General Strike*, The Cresset Press, London   John Murray, *The General Strike of 1926*, Lawrence & Wishart, London
p.130 **Mine 104**
p.131 **Distributing bread**
p.132 **Fancy dress**
p.133 **Tasting soup** R. Page Arnot, *South Wales Miners*, Cymric Federation Press, Cardiff   Margaret Morris, *The General Strike*, Penguin Books, London   Patrick Renshaw, *The General Strike*, Eyre Methuen, London   Gerard Noel, *The Great Lock-out of 1926*, Constable, London   *Red Money*, All Russian Council of Trade Unions, Labour Research Dept., London
p.134 **Russian ship** Personal recollection of W. Hodgman
p.135 **Sacco & Vanzetti** Katherine Ann Porter, *The Never Ending Wrong*, Secker & Warburg, London   *Sunday Worker*, 1 May and 7 August 1927
p.136 **Holiday coach queue** Maggie Angeloglou, *Looking back at Holidays*, E. P. Publishing, Wakefield   *Oldham Chronicle*, September 1929
p.137 *Daily Herald* Wilfred Fienburgh, *25 Momentous Years*, Odhams Press, London   Raymond Postgate, *George Lansbury*, Longmans Green & Co. London
p.138 **Women's Red Army** *The March of the Women*, Communist Party pamphlet, April 1928   *Sunday Worker*, 11 March and 6 May 1928
p.139 **Prince of Wales** John Montgomery, *The Twenties*, George Allen & Unwin, London   Michael Foot, *Aneurin Bevan Vol. 1.* MacGibbon & Kee, London   Frances Donaldson, *Edward VIII*, Weidenfeld & Nicolson, London   Christopher Hibbert, *Edward, the Uncrowned King*, McDonald & Co. Ltd. London
p.141 **North East unemployed** Wal Hannington, *Unemployed Struggles*, Lawrence & Wishart, London   *Daily Worker*, 1-8 May 1930   Personal recollection of W. Hinnigan
p.142 **Bevin/Election** Alan Bullock, *The Life and Times of Ernest Bevin, Vol. 1*, Heinemann, London   Henry Pelling, *A History of British Trade Unionism*, McMillan, London   Francis Williams, *Fifty Years March*, Odhams Press, London   Wal Hannington, *Ten Lean Years*, Victor Gollancz, London

p.143 **Cricket match** *Manor House Hospital Annual Report 1919*   V. P. V. P. E. Corney, Assistant Secretary, Manor House Hospital
p.144 **Scots marchers**
p.145 **Stockton marchers** Wal Hannington, *Ten Lean Years*, Victor Gollancz, London   Wal Hannington, *Unemployed Struggles*, Lawrence & Wishart, London   John McNair, *James Maxton*, George Allen & Unwin, London   *Daily Worker*, 1-31 October 1932
p.146 **Mat making** *Bootle Times*, 7 January 1933
p.147 **Wire drawers strike** Mick Jenkins, *Our History Pamphlet No. 60, Time and Motion Strike, Manchester 1934-7*, History Group of the Communist Party
p.148 **Hay box feeding**
p.149 **Co-op tea**
p.150 **Scots women marchers**
p.150 **First aid**
p.151 **Trafalgar Square** Wal Hannington, *Unemployed Struggles*, Lawrence & Wishart, London   Wal Hannington, *A Short History of the Unemployed*, Victor Gollancz, London   John McNair, *James Maxton*, George Allen & Unwin, London   *Daily Worker*, February and March 1934
p.152 **Jubilee/Unemployed**
p.153 **Street party** *Cheshire Year Book, 1935*   *Stockport Express*, Royal Silver Jubilee Souvenir, May 1935   *Cheshire Daily Echo*, 1, 6 and 12 May 1935   Wal Hannington, *A Short History of the Unemployed*, Victor Gollancz, London
p.155 **Welsh hunger marchers** Michael Foot, *Aneurin Bevan Vol. 1.* MacGibbon & Kee, London   *Daily Worker*, November 1936   *Reynolds News* (Hannen Swaffer) 6 November 1936
p.156 **Slum housing/Sunderland** Allen Hutt, *The Condition of the Working Class in Britain*, Martin Lawrence Ltd., London
p.157 **Fumigation** Allen Hutt, *The Condition of the Working Class in Britain*, Martin Lawrence Ltd., London   Lecture by Solly Kaye, National Museum of Labour History, February 1978   Personal recollection of the author
p.158 **Co-op divi** F. Hall & W. P. Watkins, *Co-operation*, Co-operative Union, Manchester   Personal recollections of Mrs L. Gorman and Mrs R. Gorman
p.159 **Hopping** *East London Record, No. 2*, East London History Society, 1979   *Newham Recorder*, 18 October 1979
p.160 **Cable Street**
p.161 **Trafalgar Square** Philip Piratin, *Our Flag Stays Red*, Lawrence & Wishart, London   Colin Cross, *The Fascists in Britain*, Barrie & Rockcliff, London   Sir Oswald Mosely, *My Life*, Nelson, London   Mike Power, *The Struggle Against Fascism 1931-39*, History Group of the Communist Party
p.162 **Crowds to Gala**
p.163 **Family at Gala** E. Allen, *The Durham Miners' Association, A Commemoration*, Durham area, NUM
p.164 **Women coal workers/Wigan** *List of Mines in Great Britain and the Isle of Man, 1930*. HMSO, London   National Coal Board Library
p.165 **Clothing factory** Personal recollection of R. E. Allison, Chief Executive, The Ideal Clothiers Ltd   Personal recollection of Miss M. E. Thompson
p.166 **Anti-Fascists/Belle Vue** Michael Foot, *Aneurin Bevan Vol. 1* MacGibbon & Kee, London   John Mahon, *Harry Pollitt*, Lawrence & Wishart, London   Personal recollection of Mary Eckersley
p.167 **Milk for Spain** *Daily Worker*, 2 May 1938   *Daily Herald*, 2 May 1938   *Reynolds News*, 1 May 1938
p.168 **Winter relief** Wal Hannington, *Ten Lean Years*, Victor Gollancz, London   *Daily Worker*, January 1939
p.169 **Child in gas mask** Angus Calder, *The People's War*, Jonathan Cape, London
p.171 **Evacuation** Angus Calder, *The People's War*, Jonathan Cape, London   Personal recollections of Pamela Gorman and Sarah Blackshaw
p.172 **Place signs** Angus Calder, *The People's War*, Jonathan Cape, London
p.173 **Home Guard/Bevin** Angus Calder, *The People's War*, Jonathan Cape, London   Cornwall County Council
p.174 **Underground shelterers** E. Doreen Idle, *War Over West Ham*, Faber & Faber, London   Phil Piratin, *Our Flag Stays Red*, Lawrence & Wishart, London   Angus Calder, *The People's War*, Jonathan Cape, London
p.175 **Bomb damage/Plymouth** E. Doreen Idle, *War Over West Ham*, Faber & Faber, London   Angus Calder, *The People's War*, Jonathan Cape, London
p.176 **Trafalgar Square Second Front demonstration** Michael Foot, *Aneurin Bevan Vol. 1.* MacGibbon & Kee, London   John Mahon, *Harry Pollitt*, Lawrence & Wishart, London   *Evening Standard*, 14 July 1941   *Tribune*, 13 March 1942
p.177 **Dance hall**, National Union of Tailors and Garment Workers
p.178 **Bevin boys** Trevor Evans, *Bevin*, George Allen & Unwin, London   Michael Foot, *Aneurin Bevar. Vol. 1.* MacGibbon & Kee, London   *Daily Worker*, January 1944   *Daily Express*, January 1944
p.179 **British and Russian troops** Hans Dollinger, *The Decline and Fall of Nazi Germany and Imperial Japan*, Odhams Books, London   *Daily Express*, 28 April 1945
p.180 **VE bonfire** Personal recollection of the author
p.181 **Atlee/Election victory** Francis Williams, *Fifty Years March*, Odhams Press, London   Emrys Hughes, *Sidney Silverman*, Charles Skilton, London   Emanuel Shinwell, *The Labour Story*, McDonald, London   Michael Foot, *Aneurin Bevan Vol. 2.* Davis Poynter, London
p. 182 **Hame sweet hame/Furniture unloaded** John Mahon, *Harry Pollitt*, Lawrence & Wishart, London
p. 183 **Women and children** *Daily Worker*, 11 and 13 August and September, 1946   Account from B. Hazell, C.B.E.
p. 184 **Durham Gala**
p. 185 **National Coal Board** Abe Moffat, *My Life with the Miners*, Lawrence & Wishart, London   A.W. Moyes, *The Banner Book*, Frank Graham, Newcastle upon Tyne   Annual Gala 1947, Souvenir Booklet, Durham Miners' Association
p. 186 **May Day** *Day Of Struggle*, Communist Party pamphlet, London 1949   *Daily Worker*, 1 March to 2 May 1949
p. 187 **Car Assembly/Cowley** Hugh Dalton, *High Tide and After, Memoirs*, Frederick Muller, London   Francis Williams, *Fifty Years March*, Odhams Press, London   John Montgomery, *The Fifties*, George Allen & Unwin, London

Index